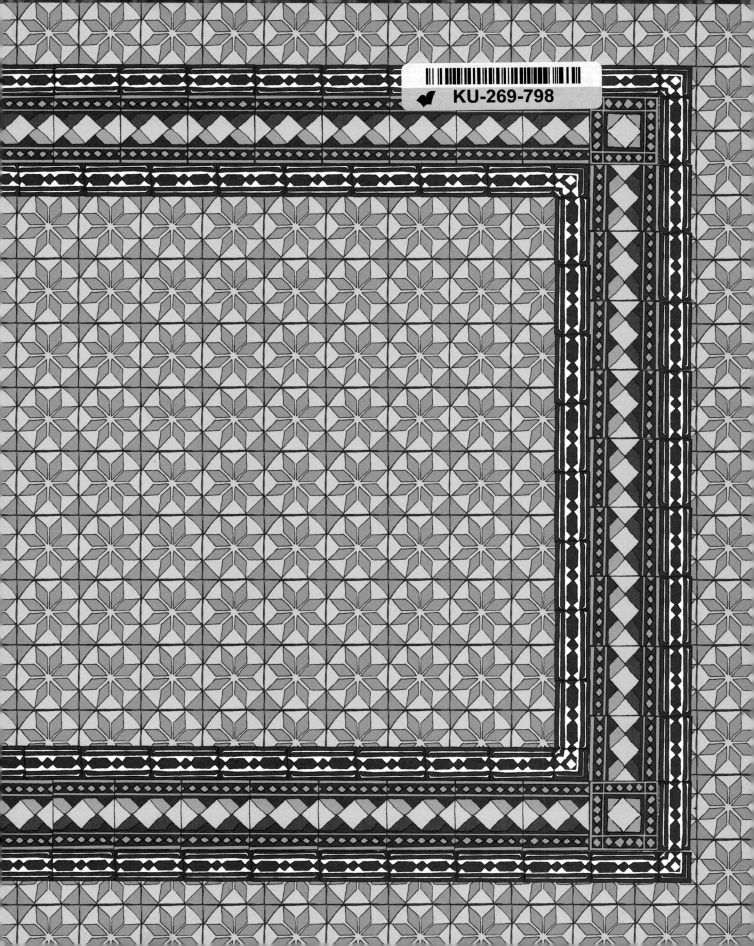

À LA MÈRE DE FAMILLE

MAISON FONDÉE EN 1761

RECIPES

FROM THE BELOVED PARISIAN CONFECTIONER

JULIEN MERCERON

PHOTOGRAPHS BY JEAN CAZALS
ILLUSTRATIONS BY SOPHIE PÉCHAUD & JULIE SERRE

CHRONICLE BOOKS
SAN FRANCISCO

preface

JANE : I remember the night you came home and told us how you'd come across the shop.

ÉTIENNE : You had just turned sixteen, and we'd celebrated your birthday in the country. Coming back to Paris, we paid a visit to Sophie and Steve.

STEVE : We already knew about the place. Sophie, you had been talking about it for some time, remember?

SOPHIE : It's the one and only time in my life that I have walked into a space and said to myself, "I want this place to be my home." Do you remember our first Christmas here?

STEVE : We were cleaned out, the shop was empty in three days! I think it was the following year when you created the famous orange bags.

ÉTIENNE : This place resembles all three of you. What I love the most is coming into the shop in December and seeing the three of you bustling around. You, Sophie, stand in the back with the chocolates. Steve is having an intense discussion with Julien, and you, Jane, man the cash register like a little girl playing shop.

JANE : Just like your children, Sophie!

SOPHIE : Well, Simon mainly, because Eliott is most interested in making homemade caramels!

JANE : Mom makes Mamie Jojo's chocolate meringues with chocolate bars from À la Mère de Famille.

ÉTIENNE : In any case, Hélène, you're our official taster.

HÉLÈNE : Everyone in the family has their own sweet. Jane's is the Gâteau Russe; Steve's is Mum's chocolate cake; Sophie, the lemon tart; and Jonathan, the coffee éclair.

STEVE : The night we first met, I brought my wife into the shop after hours.

JANE : Ha ha!

STEVE : It's true. And my son Joachim's first excursion was to come here. I have a photo of him in his pram, all the jars of bonbons behind him. He must have been a week old.

ÉTIENNE : Each of us has started our own story here. It was already a place that was loaded with history, and together each of us, with our different personalities, has built our childhood dream. Jane takes care of the chocolates with Jean-Marc. Sophie brings her spontaneity and joie de vivre to everything. The boxes, the window displays—Steve is the creative force.

STEVE : In fact, it's often Jane who has the ideas. At Christmastime, I showed her a chocolate pine wreath and she asked, "Do you think that's super Christmassy? *Super Noël?*" And that gave me the idea of the "Su-Père Noël," which we then created.

JANE : It's crazy to think that other people will be able to make Mamie Jojo's meringues now!

STEVE : I adored making this book. I re-tasted all of these treats from my childhood. We even had trouble getting a clear shot sometimes because everyone was trying to eat what was being photographed!

ÉTIENNE : This book is a true souvenir. It traces the story of À la Mère de Famille, and a bit of our history as well. I hope that your children will make these recipes, too.

La Mère et sa Famille, Paris

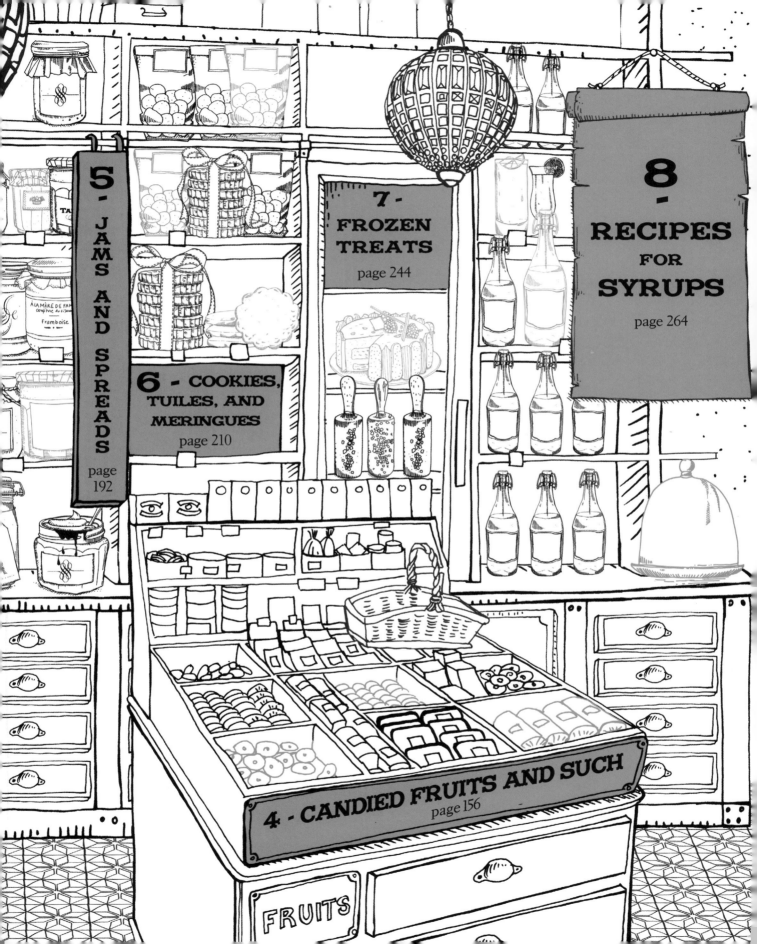

FRUITS

~A~

ACETATE *sheet*

Available from baking supply stores, acetate sheets are clear, nonstick sheets used when making chocolate shapes and decorations. Chocolate can be spread in a thin layer on the sheet, then picked up and molded. Freshly dipped chocolates can be placed on the sheet, and the chocolate will maintain its sheen.

ARRESTING *caramelization*

Dip the base of the saucepan in cold water to stop the caramelization process.

~B~

BEAT *eggs until pale*

Vigorously whisk sugar and egg yolks to make a thick, pale paste.

BUTTER, *brown*

Gently melt the butter in a saucepan; it will bubble, then foam. When all of the water evaporates and the milk solids fall to the bottom and begin to turn the color of hazelnuts, pour immediately into a cold container to arrest cooking.

BUTTER, *softened*

Butter that has been allowed to soften at room temperature is worked with a spatula until it has the consistency of a paste.

~C~

CARAMEL, *dark*

Follow the instructions for dry caramel (below), but cook the sugar to a deep, dark brown color.

CARAMEL, *diluted*

Adding warm cream to dry caramel brings down the caramel's temperature, arresting the cooking process. Be careful of spatter, and use a large pot.

CARAMEL, *dry*

Coat the bottom of a heavy saucepan with a thin layer of sugar. Place over medium heat. The sugar will melt and start to caramelize. Gradually add more sugar, being careful not to add too much at once or the mixture will seize and become lumpy.

CARAMEL, *light*

Follow the instructions for dry caramel (above), but remove the caramel from the pan as soon as it turns pale brown. Be careful: caramel darkens very quickly!

CARAMEL *sauce*

Cook the sugar without water in a heavy saucepan to make a pale caramel, then dilute with lukewarm cream.

CHOCOLATE

Chocolate comes from the processing of the cocoa bean and its combination with other ingredients. Producing good chocolate requires a rigorous process: the beans are removed from the cocoa pods, and then fermented (which is when they develop their first cocoa aromas and brown color). The beans are then sun-dried and sent to processing plants, which transform them into cocoa mass (through sorting, roasting, crushing, and grinding). The cocoa mass that results forms the basis of chocolate as we know it. This mass contains 50% cocoa butter.

Dark chocolate

Dark chocolate is made from a blend of cocoa mass, cocoa butter, sugar, and sometimes soy lecithin for stabilizing and vanilla for flavor. These ingredients are finely ground then blended, or "conched," for 122 hours to develop the smoothness and flavor of the chocolate. The quantities of each ingredient vary according to the desired percentage of cocoa. For chocolate with 70% cocoa, there is 70% cocoa mass and 30% sugar.

Milk chocolate

Milk chocolate is made from a blend of cocoa mass, cocoa butter, sugar, milk powder, and sometimes soy lecithin and vanilla.

White chocolate

White chocolate doesn't contain any cocoa mass; it is made from cocoa butter, milk powder, sugar, and sometimes soy lecithin and vanilla.

COUVERTURE

Chocolatiers like À la Mère de Famille use chocolate called "couverture," which contains at least 32% cocoa butter (the cocoa butter naturally contained in the cocoa mass plus cocoa butter added to make the chocolate). This increases the quality, and makes the chocolate more fluid for working. For the chocolate confections in this book, it is preferable to use chocolate from À la Mère de Famille or couverture chocolate, which is available from specialty baking stores and websites. Failing this, always use a chocolate with a high percentage of cacao.

CHURNING *ice cream*

This means chilling ice cream while mixing and incorporating air into it using an ice-cream maker.

~D~

DECRYSTALLIZING
sugar

At the start of the caramelization process (up to 250°F), run a wet brush around the inside of the saucepan to ensure that the sugar crystals clinging to the sides of the pan dissolve.

DIPPING
a bonbon or candied fruit in chocolate

Place the confection on a fork and dip it into tempered chocolate. Let it drain by lightly tapping the fork, then place the item on an acetate sheet. This needs to be done quickly so that the chocolate-covered bonbon doesn't stick to the fork. Keep the fork nice and clean and lightly reheat if the chocolate sets on the fork. It is generally necessary to prepare more chocolate than what is actually used for coating so that it is easy to dip the fork into it and swirl the confection around without damaging your goody.

~G~

GLAZING pastry

Brush pastry—cookies, crusts, and tart shells—with beaten egg before putting it in the oven to form a nice and shiny surface.

~M~

MOISTENING a cake

Brush syrup over all the sides of a cake with a pastry brush. Or you can dip the cake in cold syrup.

~P~

PARCHMENT-PAPER
cone

Used to form small chocolate dots for "gluing" or decorative elements. Cut parchment paper into a triangle, and then form it into a cone shape by rolling up the sides; the midpoint of the longest side of the triangle should become the tip of the cone. Secure the cone with your thumb, then fill it with melted chocolate and cut the tip off to make an opening to pipe out the chocolate. Voilà!

PULLING sugar

Pulling and folding cooked sugar several times as it cools will make it opaque and white.

~R~

RIPPLING ice cream

Lightly stir jam or coulis through softened ice cream to create a ripple effect.

~S~

325°F

SILICONE mat

Silicone mats are heat-resistant, unlike acetate sheets. You can pour hot caramel (up to 325°F) onto silicone and it will not stick.

SKIMMING jams

Removing the froth or scum that forms on the surface of jam using a skimmer.

SKIMMING syrups

Removing the froth from the surface of syrup using a skimmer.

~T~

TOASTING nuts

Toast shelled nuts for about 15 minutes in a 325°F oven. They will take on a lovely golden color. To remove the thin skin on hazelnuts and pistachios, rub them gently in a clean dish towel.

1

FINANCIERS, MADELEINES,

and cakes *à la française* are each simplicity itself, *n'est-ce pas?* It is a simplicity that borders on the sublime, as long as you are willing to learn the perfect technique and the correct proportions. Look no further: all you need to do is follow the instructions of À la Mère de Famille to the letter in order to master these classics (whether lemon, chocolate, cherry, or hazelnut is your flavor preference). Only then will you be able to offer your nearest and dearest, young and old, the most perfect of indulgences.

CAKES
GATEAUX

CAKES AND PASTRIES

A VERY NUTTY BROWNIE

MAKES 16 SMALL BROWNIES

PREPARATION TIME 15 MINUTES
BAKING TIME 30 MINUTES

1 cup plus 5 tbsp unsalted butter, plus more for greasing the pan
3½ oz 70% dark chocolate, chopped
3 eggs, separated
¾ cup light brown sugar
⅓ cup all-purpose flour
¾ cup folies de l'écureuil (page 85), roughly chopped

MAKING THE BATTER

In a double-boiler set over medium-low heat, melt together the butter and chocolate, stirring, until smooth. Remove from the heat. In a clean bowl, whip the egg whites until they hold soft peaks. In a large bowl, whisk the egg yolks with the sugar until pale and thick. Incorporate the melted chocolate (it will still be quite hot). Stir in the flour. Gently fold in the egg whites, being careful to keep the air in the mixture. Set aside a handful of the Folies de l'Écureuil; stir the rest into the batter.

BAKING

Preheat the oven to 325°F. Grease an 8-by-8-inch baking pan. Pour the batter into the prepared pan; it should be about 1½ inches deep. Scatter the reserved Folies de l'Écureuil over the top. Bake for 30 minutes, until a knife inserted into the brownie emerges with moist crumbs attached. Remove from the oven and cool on a wire rack for at least 30 minutes before cutting into small squares.

NOTE: *The nutty confection used in these brownies is aptly named:* folies de l'écureuil *translates to "a squirrel's folly."*

MORELLO CHERRY FINANCIERS

MAKES 12 FINANCIERS

PREPARATION TIME 10 MINUTES
BAKING TIME 13 MINUTES

6 tbsp unsalted butter
1¼ cups confectioners' sugar
½ cup all-purpose flour
½ cup ground almonds or almond meal
½ tsp baking powder
5 egg whites, lightly beaten
60 morello cherries in liqueur, drained

MAKING THE BATTER

In a medium saucepan over medium-low heat, gently brown the butter (see page 8). In a large mixing bowl, combine the sugar, flour, ground almonds, and baking powder. Make a well in the center of the dry ingredients, add the egg whites and the brown butter, and stir until completely incorporated.

BAKING

Preheat the oven to 375°F. Place twelve 2-inch silicone or nonstick financier molds on a baking sheet. Fill each mold just short of the rim with batter. Dot each financier with 5 cherries. Bake for about 13 minutes, until light brown and the cake springs back with lightly touched. Remove from the oven and cool on a wire rack for 10 minutes, then unmold. Eat warm, or store in an airtight container for up to 5 days.

 NOTE: *Financiers are so-called because the bakery where they were first sold was near the Paris Stock Exchange, and the shapes of these tasty cakes resemble bars of gold. And, thrifty bakers take heart: financiers are an ideal way to use up egg whites left over from other recipes. Nothing is lost!*

HAZELNUT FINANCIERS

MAKES 12 FINANCIERS

PREPARATION TIME 10 MINUTES
BAKING TIME 13 MINUTES

⅓ cup hazelnuts
6 tbsp unsalted butter
1¼ cups confectioners' sugar
½ cup all-purpose flour
½ cup ground hazelnuts
½ tsp baking powder
5 egg whites, lightly beaten

MAKING THE BATTER

Preheat the oven to 325°F. Pour the whole hazelnuts onto a baking sheet. Toast in the oven for about 10 minutes, keeping a careful eye on their color. To test doneness, break open a hazelnut: it should be golden brown inside. In a medium saucepan over medium-low heat, gently brown the butter (see page 8). In a large mixing bowl, combine the sugar, flour, ground hazelnuts, and baking powder. Make a well in the center of the dry ingredients, add the egg whites and the brown butter, and stir until completely incorporated.

BAKING

Increase the oven temperature to 375°F. Place twelve 2-inch silicone or nonstick financier molds on a baking sheet. Fill each mold just short of the rim with batter. Dot each financier with whole hazelnuts. Bake for about 15 minutes, until the cakes are light brown and spring back when lightly touched. Remove from the oven and cool on a wire rack for 10 minutes, then unmold. Eat warm.

NOTE: *Financiers will keep, stored in an airtight container, for up to 5 days.*

1761 ~ 1791

---

*

1761 ~ 1791
A SHOP WITH THE ALLURE OF A FARMHOUSE
*

1791 ~ 1807
THE FATE OF LE PÈRE DE FAMILLE

1807 ~ 1825
A FREE WOMAN

1825 ~ 1850
AT THE HEART OF ARTISTIC LIFE

1850 ~ 1895
A NEW ERA OF COOKIES

A SHOP WITH THE ALLURE OF A FARMHOUSE

One day in 1760, a young man from Coulommiers arrives in Paris with a grocer's diploma, which he has just received from the hands of the *procureur du roi.*

Fascinated by Parisian life, he wanders the streets of the capital, drawn to the rustic, festive, and carefree Faubourg-Montmartre quarter. During his first year in Paris, Pierre-Jean Bernard falls for the charms of a small farm on the corner of what is now the Rue de Provence. It consists of a three-room cottage, with an earthen floor and wooden doors, and three sheds and stables that he turns into a pretty grocery shop. The corner store quickly becomes an essential stop in Faubourg-Montmartre, which, in the years to follow, becomes a charming residential quarter that comes alive at night with balls and *boîtes.* Montmarte becomes a regular haunt of high society. Louis XV builds his recreational Hôtel des Menus Plaisirs in this part of Paris, and formal gardens bloom. Three years after making his home here, Pierre-Jean Bernard marries Marie-Catherine Fossey, and Maison Bernard is born. In 1773, the couple buys the building they run their business from, and in 1779, Pierre-Jean Bernard modernizes, expands, and develops a confectionery counter. Parisians flock to the couple's store to purchase simple, delightful, and original products, reflecting the elegant and lighthearted character of the neighborhood and its inhabitants.

Maison Bernard is a grocery store in the style of the *ancien régime.* It belongs to the apothecaries' guild and sells savory products such as vinegar, flour, wine, and hams from Bayonne, Bordeaux, and Mayence. In addition, delectable sugared almonds, jams, candied fruit, and pastries can be bought here.

1895 ~ 1920
A CHILDHOOD DREAM COME TRUE

1920 ~ 1950
THE SOUL OF THE NEIGHBORHOOD

1950 ~ 1985
ALBERT AND SUZANNE

1985 ~ 2000
A TIME FOR CHOCOLATE

2000 ~
HISTORY IN THE MAKING

SULTANA CAKE

MAKES TWO 6-BY-4-INCH CAKES OR ONE 9-BY-4-INCH CAKE
PREPARATION TIME 15 MINUTES
BAKING TIME 45 MINUTES

BATTER

flour .... 1½ cups
ground almonds or almond meal .... ¼ cup
baking powder...1 tsp
sultanas or golden raisins .... 1½ cups
dark rum .... 4 tsp
unsalted butter, softened..................................... ½ cup plus 2 tbsp
confectioners' sugar .... 1¼ cups
eggs, room temperature 3

SYRUP

water .... 1 cup plus 2 tbsp
superfine sugar .... ¼ cup
dark rum .... 1 tbsp

MAKING THE BATTER

Sift the flour, ground almonds, and baking powder into a small bowl. Set aside. In another small bowl, soak the sultanas in the rum for at least 15 minutes. In a large mixing bowl, cream together the butter and confectioners' sugar until smooth. Add the eggs one at a time, beating constantly, until they are well incorporated. Fold in the flour, then the sultanas and their liquid.

BAKING

Preheat the oven to 400°F. Line two 6-by-4-inch or one 9-by-4-inch loaf pan(s) with parchment paper. Pour the batter into the prepared pan. Bake for 5 minutes, then make a lengthwise incision in the top of the cake with a sharp knife. Lower the oven temperature to 300°F, then return the cake to the oven for about 40 minutes, until the cake is golden-brown and a knife inserted into the middle comes out clean. Remove from the oven and cool in the pan on a wire rack for 10 minutes, then turn the cake out of the pan.

MAKING THE SYRUP

In a small saucepan, combine the water, sugar, and rum. Bring to a boil, then remove from the heat and, while cake and syrup are still warm, use a pastry brush to moisten the cake with the syrup. Cool completely before serving. (The cake will keep in an airtight container for up to 5 days.)

PISTACHIO CAKE

MAKES TWO 6-BY-4-INCH CAKES OR ONE 9-BY-4-INCH CAKE

PREPARATION TIME 15 MINUTES
BAKING TIME 40 MINUTES

4 eggs
1½ cups sugar
⅓ cup whipping cream, warmed
3½ tbsp pistachio paste
1¾ cups all-purpose flour, sifted
1½ tsp baking powder
6 tbsp unsalted butter, melted
Handful of chopped pistachios

MAKING THE BATTER

In a large mixing bowl, whisk the eggs and sugar until the mixture is pale and thick. Add the cream and pistachio paste and whisk until combined. Fold in the flour and baking powder. Finally, stir in the butter. The batter should be smooth and shiny.

BAKING

Preheat the oven to 400°F. Line two 6-by-4-inch or one 9-by-4-inch loaf pan(s) with parchment paper. Pour the batter into the prepared pan and scatter the chopped pistachios over the top. Bake for 5 minutes, then make a lengthwise incision in the top of the cake with a sharp knife. Lower the oven temperature to 300°F, then return the cake to the oven for about 35 minutes, until the cake is golden-brown and a knife inserted into the middle comes out clean. Remove from the oven and cool in the pan on a wire rack for 10 minutes, then turn the cake out of the pan. Cool completely before serving. (The cake will keep in an airtight container for up to 3 days.)

CHEF'S TIP: *To keep the cake moister, wrap it in plastic wrap as soon as it comes out of the oven and allow it to cool like that.*

CHOCOLATE CAKE

MAKES TWO 6-BY-2-INCH CAKES OR ONE 9-BY-4-INCH CAKE

PREPARATION TIME 15 MINUTES
BAKING TIME 40 MINUTES

3 eggs
½ cup sugar
3 tbsp honey
½ cup whipping cream
50 g 1½ oz dark chocolate (70% cocoa)

¾ cup all-purpose flour, sifted
⅔ cup ground almonds
1½ tsp baking powder
3 tbsp unsweetened cocoa powder
4 tbsp unsalted butter, melted

MAKING THE BATTER

In a large mixing bowl, whisk the eggs, sugar, and honey until the mixture is pale and thick. In a medium saucepan, heat the cream until just under the boiling point, then add the chocolate and stir until smooth. Remove from the heat, cool slightly, then stir the chocolate mixture into the egg mixture. Add the flour, ground almonds, baking powder, and cocoa and fold until combined. Stir in the melted butter. The batter should be smooth and shiny.

BAKING

Preheat the oven to 400°F. Line two 6-by-2-inch or one 9-by-4-inch loaf pan(s) with parchment paper. Pour the batter into the prepared pan. Bake for 5 minutes, then make a lengthwise incision in the top of the cake with a sharp knife. Lower the oven temperature to 300°F, then return the cake to the oven for about 35 minutes until a knife inserted into the middle of the cake comes out clean. Remove from the oven and cool in the pan on a wire rack for 10 minutes, then turn the cake out of the pan. Cool completely before serving.

 CHEF'S TIP: *It is not essential to use couverture chocolate for this chocolate cake. A dark chocolate with a high percentage of cocoa will work perfectly.*

CUSTOMER PORTRAITS:
THOMAS CHATTERTON WILLIAMS

OCCUPATION . . . . Writer
NEIGHBORHOOD . . . . Brooklyn
MOST VISITED STORE . . . . Rue Cler
FIRST VISIT . . . . One year ago

FREQUENCY OF VISITS . . . . . . Once a week when in Paris
FAVORITE CHOCOLATE . . . . Milk
CHOCOLATE CONSUMPTION . . . . Impossible to stop!

1
WHEN DO YOU VISIT THE STORE?
In the afternoon, when I want a coffee and some bonbons. I visit without fail every time I'm in France.

2
WHAT IS YOUR GREATEST INDULGENCE?
A glass of Champagne.

3
WHAT KIND OF TREATS DO YOU LIKE TO SHARE?
Lemon cake. It's delicious, but too big to eat myself!

4
THE TREAT YOU ENJOY ALONE?
Caramels!

5
THE MOST ROMANTIC TREAT?
Champagne and, above all, chocolate.

6
THE MOST AMUSING TREAT?
I think eating well is a very serious thing.

7
DESCRIBE A PERFECT MOMENT LINKED TO A TREAT FROM À LA MÈRE DE FAMILLE.
The time I tasted all of the flavors in the store. After that, it was impossible to eat anything else for the rest of the day.

8
IF LA MÈRE WERE TO GIVE YOU A PRESENT, WHAT WOULD YOU LIKE IT TO BE?
Champagne and pâtes de fruits.

9
WHAT DOES À LA MÈRE DE FAMILLE REPRESENT FOR YOU?
Tradition, and the highest quality possible.

10
WHAT DO YOU THINK SHOULD BE THE MOTTO OF À LA MÈRE DE FAMILLE?
"Life is sweet."

11
WHAT IS THE SECRET TO ITS ENDURING SUCCESS?
Love.

12
WHAT MAKES THE SHOP DIFFERENT FROM OTHERS LIKE IT?
The fact that it is run by a family that loves chocolates—loves creating and eating chocolates—and not by a company that is only interested in selling product.

13
DESCRIBE YOUR FIRST ENCOUNTER.
I went there with my wife one cold January day. I bought some bonbons for my mother and fell in love with the store.

14
WHAT DOES THE STORE'S HISTORY EVOKE FOR YOU?
The idea that À la Mère de Famille existed in Napoléon's time!

15
WHY DO YOU LOVE À LA MÈRE DE FAMILLE?
Above all, for its orange bags!

LEMON CAKE

MAKES TWO 6-BY-2-INCH CAKES OR ONE 9-BY-4-INCH CAKE

PREPARATION TIME 15 MINUTES
BAKING TIME 40 MINUTES

FOR THE BATTER
1½ cups sugar
4 lemons, washed
½ cup whipping cream
4 eggs
1¾ cups all-purpose flour
1½ tsp baking powder
5 tbsp unsalted butter, melted

FOR THE SYRUP
1 cup water
½ cup sugar
5 tsp lemon juice

¼ cup candied lemon peel

MAKING THE BATTER

Put the sugar in a large mixing bowl and grate the zest from the lemons into the sugar. This captures the flavorful lemon oils. In a small saucepan over low heat, warm the cream. Juice the lemons and set aside the 5 tsp needed to make the syrup. Add the eggs to the lemony sugar and whisk until the mixture becomes pale and thick. Stir in the warm cream, then sift in the flour and baking powder and fold to incorporate. Finally, add the melted butter and stir to make a smooth, shiny batter.

BAKING

Preheat the oven to 400°F. Lightly grease and line two 6-by-2-inch or one 9-by-4-inch pan(s) with parchment paper. Pour the batter into the prepared pan. Bake for 5 minutes, then make a lengthwise incision in the top of the cake with a sharp knife. Lower the oven temperature to 300°F, then return the cake to the oven to bake for about 35 minutes, until a knife inserted into the middle of the cake comes out clean. Remove from the oven, turn the cakes out of the pans, and allow to cool on a wire rack.

MAKING THE SYRUP

In a small saucepan, bring the sugar, water, and lemon juice to a boil. Remove from the heat and allow to cool. While the cake and syrup are still warm, use a pastry brush to moisten the cake with all of the syrup. Finish decorating the cake by placing strips of candied lemon peel on top.

STORAGE: *Thanks to the lemon syrup, these cakes stay moist for several days. They are ideal for wrapping and taking to the country for a picnic, or enjoying for afternoon tea or as a weekend dessert.*

ORANGE-CHOCOLATE CAKE

MAKES TWO 6-BY-2-INCH CAKES OR ONE 9-BY-4-INCH CAKE

PREPARATION TIME 15 MINUTES
BAKING TIME 40 MINUTES

FOR THE BATTER
1½ cups sugar
2 oranges, washed
3 eggs
½ cup cream, warmed
1¾ cups all-purpose flour
1½ tsp baking powder
5 tbsp unsalted butter, melted
½ cup dark chocolate chips

FOR THE SYRUP
½ cup water
½ cup sugar
Juice of 2 oranges

sliced candied orange peel (page 102),
for decorating

MAKING THE BATTER

Put the sugar in a large mixing bowl and grate the zest from the oranges into the sugar. This captures the flavorful orange oils. (Reserve the oranges for the syrup.) Add the eggs to the sugar and whisk until the mixture becomes pale and thick. Add the warm cream and stir to combine. Sift in the flour and baking powder and fold to incorporate. Finally, add the melted butter and most of the chocolate chips, reserving a few to decorate the top. Stir to make a smooth, shiny batter.

BAKING

Preheat the oven to 400°F. Lightly grease and flour, or line with parchment paper, two 6-by-2-inch or 9-by-4-inch loaf pan(s). Pour the batter into the prepared pan, scatter the reserved chocolate chips over the top, and bake for 5 minutes. Remove the cake from the oven and make a lengthwise incision in the top using a knife. Reduce the oven temperature to 300°F and return the cake to the oven to bake for about 35 minutes, or until the blade of a knife comes out clean when inserted into the center of the cakes. Remove from the oven, turn the cakes out of the pans, and allow to cool on a wire rack.

MAKING THE SYRUP

Juice the reserved oranges. In a small saucepan, bring the sugar, water, and orange juice to a boil. Boil until thick and syrupy, about 7 minutes. Remove from the heat and allow to cool. While the cake and syrup are still warm, use a pastry brush to moisten the cake with all of the syrup, brushing the top, bottom, and sides. Finish decorating the cake by placing strips of candied orange peel on top.

PAIN D'ÉPICE

MAKES THREE 6-BY-2-INCH CAKES

PREPARATION TIME 15 MINUTES
BAKING TIME 40 MINUTES

1 cup honey, preferably fir honey
½ cup whole milk
A pinch of salt
1½ tsp ground cinnamon
1 tsp ground star anise
1¾ cups rye flour

1½ cup whole wheat flour
2 tsp baking powder
3 eggs
½ cup plus 2 tbsp unsalted butter, melted
2 cups diced candied orange peel (page 102)

MAKING THE BATTER

In a medium saucepan over medium heat, combine the honey, milk, salt, cinnamon, and star anise. Bring to a simmer, stirring to combine, then remove from the heat and allow to infuse for 15 minutes. Meanwhile, sift together both flours and the baking powder into a large mixing bowl. In a separate bowl, mix the eggs with the spiced milk mixture and the butter. Add to the dry ingredients, mix well, then fold in the orange peel.

BAKING

Preheat the oven to 300°F. Line three 6-by-2-inch loaf pans with parchment paper. Pour the batter into the prepared pans. Bake for about 40 minutes, until the cakes are deep golden and the blade of a knife inserted into the center comes out clean. Remove from the oven and cool in the pans on a wire rack for at least 30 minutes, then turn the cakes out of the pans. Cool completely before serving. (Store in an airtight container for up to 5 days.)

 CHEF'S TIP: *You can use other spices to flavor these cakes—try adding ground coriander, fresh grated nutmeg, seeds from a vanilla bean, or some ground cardamom to the spiced milk infusion. The loaves make lovely bread pudding or French toast.*

1791 ~ 1807

1761 ~ 1791
A SHOP WITH THE ALLURE OF A FARMHOUSE

1791 ~ 1807
THE FATE OF LE PÉRE DE FAMILLE
*

1807 ~ 1825
A FREE WOMAN

1825 ~ 1850
AT THE HEART OF ARTISTIC LIFE

1850 ~ 1895
A NEW ERA OF COOKIES

THE
FATE
OF LE PÈRE DE
FAMILLE

The Bernards prosper, and their three daughters expand the Faubourg-Montmartre store.

Many people, including aristocrats, artists, painters, musicians, and poets, are attracted to the rustic charm of this district of Paris. They settle into the neoclassical homes of the neighborhood. Citizens of Paris talk about the cultural avant-gardism of the Rue Faubourg-Montmartre, and of its freedom and gaiety. In the midst of this joyful effervescence and at the height of revolutionary fever, Jeanne, the second of the daughters, marries Jean-Marie Bridauld, the son of a great family of grocers from the Rue Saint-Antoine. The young couple takes a shine to the candy store, and when they take it over in 1791,

it is rebaptized Maison Bridauld. During this time, there is a paradigm shift in French confectionary arts, and the old, aristocratic establishments and labels on the Rue des Lombards begin to feel fusty and outmoded. Maison Bridauld takes root in the wake of a new generation of democratic confectionary arts. As the pleasures of gastronomy are associated with liberty, and the French discover the art of entertaining, the sweetmeats and other fashionable treats of Maison Bridauld become a paradise for gourmands. After the tragic deaths of Jeanne and her two youngest daughters, Jean-Marie continues to run the store with his eldest daughter. He eventually remarries, to the beautiful Marie-Adélaïde Delamarte who becomes the emblematic figure of À la Mère de Famille.

Legend has it that in 1793, smack in the middle of the French Revolution, the mother superior of a neighboring convent took refuge in the store's cellar to escape the condemnation of a mob. To thank the Bridauld family for protecting her, she offered them a magical formula for a sweet syrup. This potion was made until the end of World War II, when the recipe was mysteriously lost.

1895 ~ 1920	1920 ~ 1950	1950 ~ 1985	1985 ~ 2000	2000 ~
A CHILDHOOD DREAM COME TRUE	THE SOUL OF THE NEIGHBORHOOD	ALBERT AND SUZANNE	A TIME FOR CHOCOLATE	HISTORY IN THE MAKING

ROYAL BISCUIT
WITH CANDIED FRUIT

MAKES 1 CAKE
PREPARATION TIME 15 MINUTES
BAKING TIME 50 MINUTES

honey, preferably fir or chestnut honey.....................................¾ cup
whole milk ....½ cup
ground cinnamon ....1½ tsp
ground ginger ....1½ tsp
ground aniseed ....1½ tsp
ground star anise ....1 tsp
rye flour...1 cup
whole-wheat flour...1 cup
baking powder..1¼ tsp
unsalted butter, melted..6 tbsp
candied fruit, diced ....2¼ cups

MAKING THE BATTER

In a medium saucepan over medium heat, combine the honey, milk, and spices. Bring to a simmer, stirring to combine, then remove from the heat and allow to infuse for at least 15 minutes. Meanwhile, sift together both flours and the baking powder into a large mixing bowl. Whisk in the spiced milk mixture, followed by the butter. Fold in the candied fruit.

BAKING

Preheat the oven to 300°F. Line the bottom of a 6-inch springform pan with parchment paper and place on a baking sheet. Pour the batter into the prepared pan. Bake for about 50 minutes, until the cake is deep golden and the blade of a knife inserted into the center comes out clean. Remove from the oven and transfer to a wire rack. Cool for 15 minutes, then remove the pan sides to cool completely before serving.

MADELEINES

MAKES 24 MADELEINES

PREPARATION TIME 10 MINUTES
BAKING TIME 7 MINUTES

2 cups all-purpose flour
1½ tsp baking powder
1 cup sugar
2½ tsp vanilla sugar
4 eggs
½ cup plus 1 tbsp unsalted butter, melted,
plus more for greasing the molds
3½ tbsp whole milk

MAKING THE BATTER

Sift the flour and baking powder into a large mixing bowl. In a medium bowl, combine sugar, vanilla sugar, and eggs. In a small mixing bowl, stir together the butter and milk. Make a well in the flour mixture and pour in the egg mixture; whisk until just combined. Whisk in the milk mixture. Press plastic wrap against the surface of the batter and refrigerate for at least 1 hour and up to overnight.

BAKING

Preheat the oven to 375°F. Butter two 12-well madeleine pans. Divide the batter among the wells of the prepared pans and bake for about 7 minutes, until the cakes spring back when touched lightly. Remove from the oven and immediately turn the madeleines out of the pans and onto a wire rack.

CHEF'S TIP: *To give your madeleines a rounded "hump", you need to open the oven door and close it quickly. Do this when the batter is cooked around the outside but not yet in the center. Cool slightly, then eat immediately, or store in an airtight container for up to a week.*

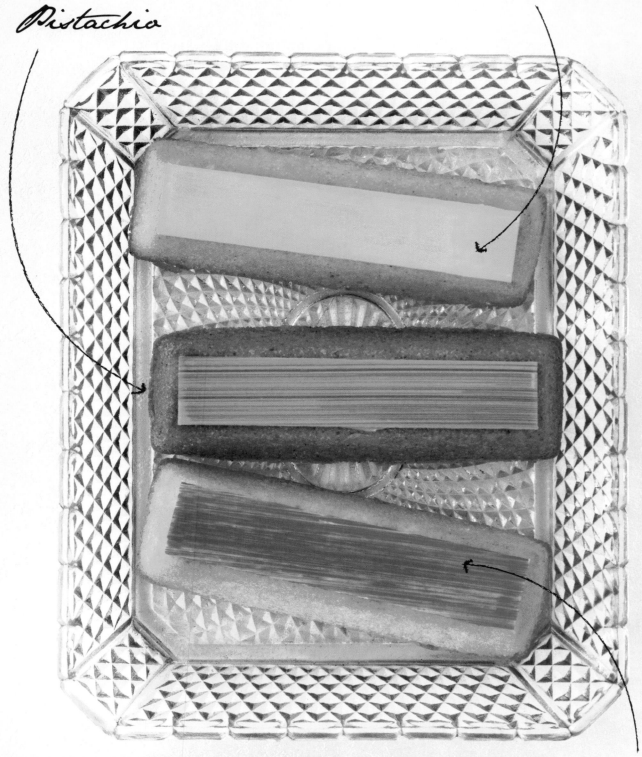

Pistachio

Lemon

Raspberry

- AMANTS FROM À LA MÈRE DE FAMILLE -

Milk chocolate — Coffee — Dark chocolate

LEMON AMANTS

MAKES 10 CAKES

PREPARATION TIME 1 HOUR

For the cakes
6 egg whites, lightly beaten
1⅔ cups confectioners' sugar
¾ cup ground almonds
½ cup all-purpose flour
Grated zest of 1 lemon
7 tbsp unsalted butter, melted

For the filling
3½ tbsp lemon juice
1 egg
⅓ cup granulated sugar
5 tbsp unsalted butter, cut into cubes

For the topping
4 oz white chocolate, chopped
Yellow food coloring for chocolate*

MAKING THE CAKES

Preheat the oven to 350°F. Lightly grease ten 2-by-2-inch ingot-shaped molds and set them on a baking sheet. In a large mixing bowl, whisk together the egg whites, confectioners' sugar, ground almonds, and flour. Stir in the lemon zest, then the melted butter. Pour the batter into the prepared molds, filling them just to the rim (about 1¾ oz of batter per mold). Bake for about 12 minutes, until lightly golden. Remove from the oven, unmold the cakes, and cool on a wire rack.

MAKING THE FILLING

In a nonreactive saucepan over high heat, bring the lemon juice to a boil. Meanwhile, in a medium bowl, whisk together the egg and granulated sugar. Reduce the heat to medium, then whisk the egg mixture into the lemon juice. Cook for 2 minutes until thickened. Stir in the butter, cool, then refrigerate.

MAKING THE TOPPING

In a double boiler, melt the white chocolate, add a dab of yellow food coloring, and temper the chocolate (see page 46). Spread the tempered chocolate in a thin layer onto a 19-by-24-inch acetate sheet. Let cool until almost set, at least 10 minutes, then cut into 10 rectangles the same size as the molds. Place the chocolate rectangles—still on the acetate—between two baking sheets and refrigerate for 10 minutes, until firm. Make a line of lemon filling on the top of each cake. Invert a chocolate rectangle onto each and peel off the acetate.

* *Unlike food coloring for sugar, which is water-soluble, food coloring for chocolate comes in fat-soluble powder form. It may also come in the form of colored cocoa butter.*

AND OTHER AMANTS

RASPBERRY

FOR THE CAKES
6 egg whites, lightly beaten
1²⁄₃ cups confectioners' sugar
¾ cup ground almonds
½ cup all-purpose flour
7 tbsp unsalted butter, melted

FOR THE FILLING
⅓ cup raspberry pulp
½ cup granulated sugar

FOR THE TOPPING
4 oz white chocolate, chopped
Red food coloring for chocolate*

MAKING THE CAKES
Preheat the oven to 350°F. Lightly grease ten 2-by-2-inch ingot-shaped molds and set them on a baking sheet. In a large mixing bowl, whisk together the egg whites, confectioners' sugar, ground almonds, and flour. Add the melted butter and stir to combine. Pour the batter into the prepared molds (about 1¾ ounces of batter per mold). Bake for 12 minutes. Remove from the oven, unmold the cakes, and cool on a wire rack.

MAKING THE FILLING
Put the raspberry pulp and granulated sugar in a small saucepan, bring to a boil, and cook like a jam until thickened. Remove from the heat and refrigerate until needed.

MAKING THE TOPPING
Make the chocolate rectangle topping and fill and assemble the cakes following the instructions on the facing page, but add red food coloring instead of yellow before tempering the chocolate.

CHOCOLATE

FOR THE CAKES
6 egg whites, lightly beaten
1²⁄₃ cups confectioners' sugar
¾ cup ground almonds
½ cup all-purpose flour
⅓ cup unsweetened cocoa powder
7 tbsp unsalted butter, melted

FOR THE FILLING
½ cup whipping cream
3 oz dark chocolate (70% cocoa), chopped
2 tbsp unsalted butter

FOR THE TOPPING
4 oz dark chocolate, chopped

MAKING THE CAKES
Preheat the oven to 350°F. Lightly grease ten 2-by-2-inch ingot-shaped molds and set them on a baking sheet. In a large mixing bowl, whisk together the egg whites, confectioners' sugar, ground almonds, flour, and cocoa powder. Add the melted butter and stir to combine. Pour the batter into the prepared molds (about 1¾ ounces of batter per mold). Bake for 12 minutes. Remove from the oven, unmold the cakes, and cool on a wire rack.

MAKING THE FILLING
Put the chocolate into a heatproof bowl. In a small saucepan, bring the cream to just under a boil, then pour over the chocolate. Stir to melt the chocolate and make a ganache—it should be smooth and shiny. Stir in the butter, then refrigerate until needed.

MAKING THE TOPPING
Make the chocolate rectangle topping and fill and assemble the cakes following the instructions on the facing page, but add red food coloring instead of yellow before tempering the chocolate.

2

AT À LA MÈRE DE FAMILLE,
chocolate confections like Biarritz rochers and
Toucans can take you on a little holiday, while
chocolate eggs and lollipops for swirling into hot
milk might take you back to a happy childhood.
In this chapter, we include instructions from
a chocolatier on how to temper chocolate and
make your own chocolate bar. But the art of the
chocolatier is not one that can be improvised,
so before you start, what you need to succeed is
couverture chocolate for optimal texture, a digital
instant-read thermometer for tempering the
chocolate, and an acetate sheet to help produce
smooth and shiny chocolate treats.

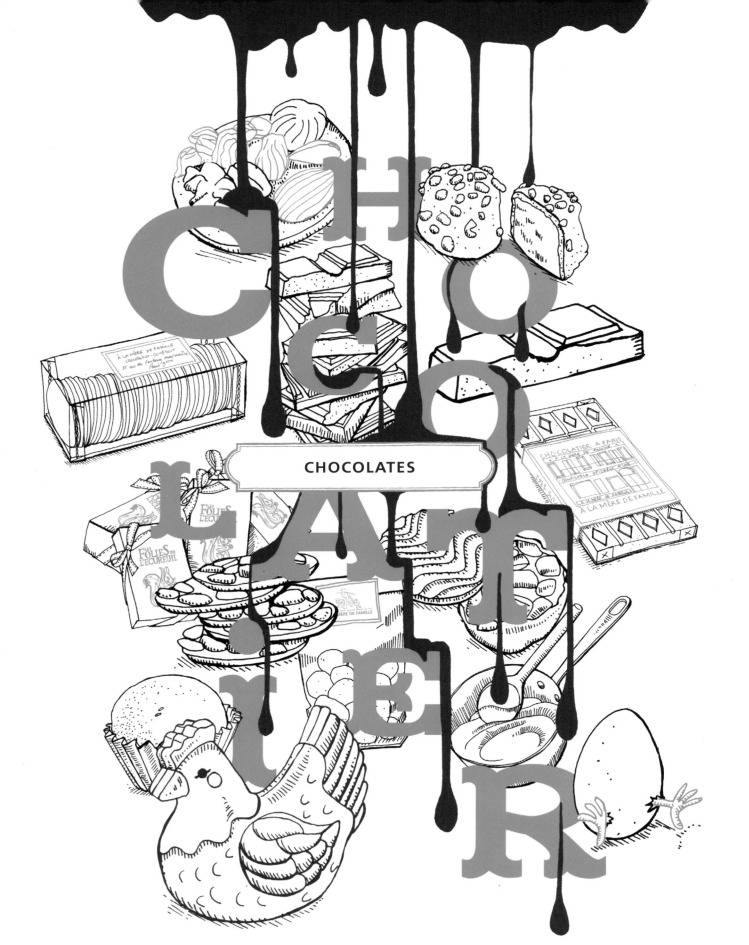

CHOCOLATES

TEMPERING CHOCOLATE

PREPARATION TIME 15 MINUTES

1⅓ lbs couverture chocolate
or 1⅓ lbs dark chocolate (70% cocoa), chopped

Place two-thirds of the chocolate in a heatproof bowl over a saucepan of simmering water, making sure the base of the bowl does not touch the water (this setup is called a "double boiler"). Allow the chocolate to melt, stirring occasionally, until it reaches its correct melting temperature (see below). Remove the bowl from the heat, add the remaining chocolate, and combine with a spatula. As the chocolate melts, allow the temperature of the mixture to fall to the cooling temperature. Reheat the chocolate to the "using temperature" (see below) over the saucepan of simmering water. To check the temper of the chocolate, dip the point of a knife into it—the chocolate should set quickly and evenly at room temperature. When working with tempered chocolate, make sure you keep it at "using temperature" or the chocolate will lose its temper.

DARK CHOCOLATE
Melting temperature: 120°F
Cooling temperature: 85°F
Using temperature: 90°F

MILK CHOCOLATE
Melting temperature: 115°F
Cooling temperature: 80°F
Using temperature: 90°F

WHITE CHOCOLATE OR COLORED CHOCOLATE
Melting temperature: 105°F
Cooling temperature: 80°F
Using temperature: 85°F

*The techniques of
Julien Merceron*

PRALINE PASTE

1¾ cups almonds or hazelnuts, or a mixture of both
1 cup plus 2 tbsp sugar

TOASTING THE NUTS
Preheat the oven to 325°F. Place the nuts on a baking sheet and toast for 10 minutes, keeping a careful eye on their color. Remove from the oven, allow to cool, then rub the nuts in a clean dish towel to remove the skins.

MAKING THE CARAMEL
Put the sugar in a saucepan and make a dark caramel, following the instructions on page 8. Add the toasted nuts to the caramel and stir to combine. Pour the caramel and nuts onto a silicone mat and allow to cool to room temperature.

PROCESSING
Break the caramel into small pieces. Place about one-third of the pieces in a food processor, process to a powder, and then continue processing—as the powder heats up, the oils contained in the nuts are released, and a praline paste slowly forms. Transfer to a container and repeat with the remaining caramel pieces. The praline paste can be stored in an airtight container at 65°F, away from moisture. If the praline paste is stored for too long, the oil will rise to the surface. You will then need to process it again before using. This praline paste is used as a base for a variety of chocolate confections. It can also be used to flavor creams and ice creams.

VARIATION: *You can use other nuts to make the praline paste—try using walnuts, pistachios, or cashews. You can also add coffee or spices during cooking to make flavored praline pastes.*

FLORENTINES

PREPARATION AND BAKING TIME 1 HOUR
CHILLING TIME 15 MINUTES

¾ cup sugar
⅓ cup whipping cream
3½ tbsp honey
½ cup candied orange peel (page 102)
or candied kumquats (page 182), diced
1½ cups sliced almonds
5 oz dark chocolate (70% cocoa), chopped
or good-quality milk chocolate

MAKING THE BASE

Preheat the oven to 325°F. Put the sugar, cream, and honey in a saucepan and heat, stirring, until the mixture registers 245°F on an instant-read thermometer. Stir in the candied orange peel and the almonds. Remove from the heat. Spoon the mixture into forty 2-inch silicone tartlet molds and bake until the florentines are a beautiful golden color, about 6 minutes. Remove from the oven, turn out immediately from the molds, and allow to cool on a wire rack.

APPLYING THE CHOCOLATE

Temper the chocolate (see page 46). Using a spoon, coat the bottom of each florentine with a thin layer of tempered chocolate. Refrigerate, chocolate-side up, for 15 minutes to set before serving. (Florentines can be stored for up to 10 days in an airtight container at room temperature.)

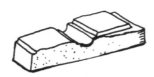

 CHEF'S TIP: *Even though your florentines might not turn out perfectly round and even on the first try, you will find they are still much better than the ones from the supermarket — it's guaranteed!*

EASTER CHOCOLATE MEDLEY

MAKES ABOUT 50 PIECES

PREPARATION TIME 20 MINUTES
CHILLING TIME 30 MINUTES

7 oz good-quality dark, milk, or white chocolate
(preferably couverture)

FILLING THE MOLDS
Wipe about 50 small (about 1⅜-inch) chocolate molds in the shapes of seashells, fish, and crustaceans with a clean kitchen towel. Fit a piping bag with a ⅛-inch plain tip. Temper the chocolate (see page 46). Fill the piping bag with the tempered chocolate and fill each mold. Tap to bring any air bubbles to the surface and wipe off any excess chocolate with a spatula.

REFRIGERATION
Place chocolate molds in the refrigerator for 30 minutes to set, then turn the chocolates out of the molds. Store the chocolates in an airtight container in a cool place (ideally 65°F) and away from moisture for up to 1 month.

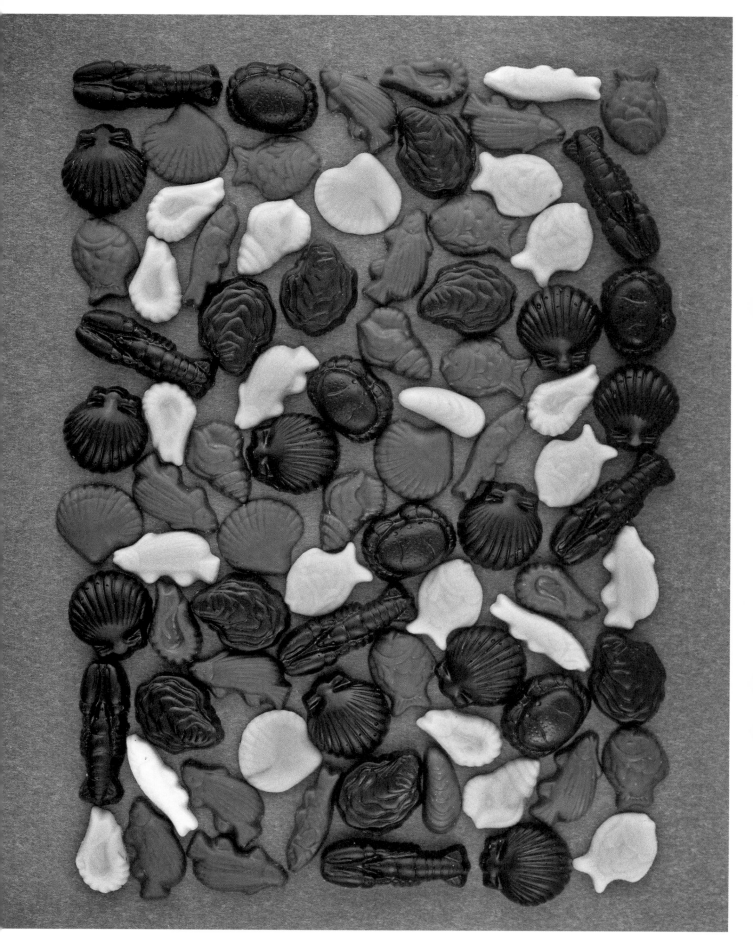

THE CHOCOLATE EGG

MAKES ONE 4¼-OZ EGG

PREPARATION TIME 1 HOUR
RESTING TIME 30 MINUTES

7 oz good-quality dark, milk, or white chocolate
(preferably couverture), chopped

PREPARING THE HALF SHELLS

Wipe a 3- to 4-inch egg mold with a clean kitchen towel. Temper the chocolate (see page 46). Pour the tempered chocolate into the mold to coat the sides, tap to bring any air bubbles to the surface, then turn the mold upside down and pour the excess back into the bowl used for tempering. Place the mold upside down on a sheet of parchment paper. Wait for the chocolate to set—about 15 minutes at 65°F. Detach the egg mold from the parchment paper and scrape off any excess chocolate with a knife or small spatula. Repeat the process to coat the mold with a second layer of chocolate. Set the mold upside down on the parchment paper after scraping off the excess chocolate.

REFRIGERATION

Refrigerate the mold for 20 minutes until the chocolate sets. Carefully remove the egg halves from the mold.

ASSEMBLING THE EGG

To assemble the egg, set a flat-bottomed saucepan over low heat for 5 minutes until warm, remove from the heat, and invert so the bottom faces up. Lightly melt the open side of each half-shell on the warm pan bottom. Bring the two halves together, aligning them carefully—the melted chocolate around the edges will act as glue.

 CHEF'S TIP: *Be very careful when preparing this chocolate egg! Warm fingertips placed on the surface of the egg will leave their mark. To prevent this from happening, wear rubber gloves when handling the egg or cover the egg with plastic wrap.*

THE CHOCOLATE EGG

{ MADE STEP-BY-STEP }

1

STEP 1
~

Pour the tempered chocolate into the egg mold and pour off the excess chocolate.

2

STEP 2
~

Place the mold upside down on a sheet of parchment paper.

3

STEP 3
~

Scrape off the excess chocolate with smooth knife or small spatula. Repe steps 1 through 3 and refrigerate.

6

STEP 6

~

Adhere the two halves together.

4

STEP 4

~

Remove the egg from the mold.

5

STEP 5

~

Assemble the egg by lightly melting the flat side of each half-shell on the base of a heated saucepan.

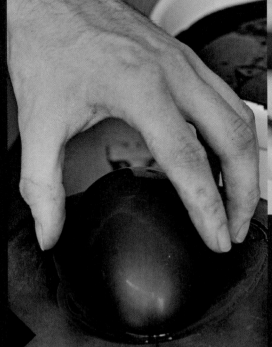

THE END

THE CHOCOLATE HEN

MAKES ONE 8-OZ HEN

PREPARATION TIME 3 HOURS
RESTING TIME 30 MINUTES

7 oz good-quality dark, milk, or white chocolate
(preferably couverture), chopped
2 oz marzipan
Yellow and red liquid food colorings

MAKING THE CHOCOLATE HEN

Draw and cut out cardboard templates for the hen's comb, tail, wattle, and wings. Temper the chocolate (see page 46). Wipe a 5- to 6-inch egg mold and two $3\frac{1}{8}$-inch hemisphere molds with a clean kitchen towel. Mold a half-egg for the base and two hemispheres for the body of the hen, making two layers of chocolate for each part (see page 54). Spread a $\frac{1}{4}$-inch-thick layer of tempered chocolate on an acetate sheet placed on a baking sheet and wait for the chocolate to start to set. Using the cardboard templates and a knife with a thin blade, cut out a comb, tail, wattle, and two wings. Cover the chocolate shapes with a sheet of parchment, then place another baking sheet on top to press them down: this will prevent the chocolate from warping as it cools. Place in the refrigerator for 30 minutes to set.

ASSEMBLING THE HEN

Unmold and peel off all of the components. Heat the base of a flat-bottomed saucepan. Lightly melt the open side of the two hemispheres on the warm pan bottom. Bring the two halves together, aligning them carefully—the melted chocolate around the edges will act as glue. Set aside for a few minutes to set. Attach the sphere to the half-egg (see page 60). Attach the comb and the wattle using a line of melted chocolate as glue. Heat the wings and the tail where they will attach to the body, then attach them with a dab of melted chocolate.

FINISHING

Color one-third of the marzipan yellow, another one-third red, and leave the remainder uncolored. Make the beak by forming the yellow ball of marzipan into a cone shape and attaching it above the wattle. Make the eyes by flattening two small balls of uncolored marzipan and attach them above the beak. Make the feet by pinching together three small pointed sausages of red marzipan at one end. Attach them to the base of the sphere. Finally, make two dots of dark chocolate on the eyes for the pupils.

THE CHOCOLATE HEN

{ MADE STEP-BY-STEP }

1

STEP 1
~
Spread a ¼-inch-thick layer of chocolate on an acetate sheet and wait for the chocolate to start to set.

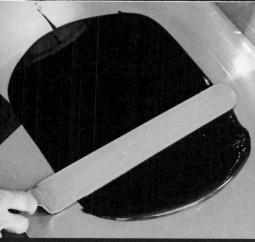

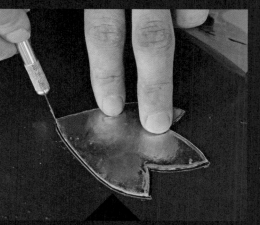

3

STEP 3
~
Assemble the body by lightly melting the edge of the open side of each hemisphere on the base of an inverted heated pan.

2

STEP 2
~
Using the templates and a thin-bladed knife, cut out all the pieces needed for assembly (comb, tail, wattle, and two wings).

4

STEP 4
~
Assemble the hemispheres and set aside for a few minutes.

5

STEP 5
~

Use a heated spatula to lightly melt the top of the egg half.

6

STEP 6
~

Attach the sphere to the egg half.

7

STEP 7
~

Lightly heat the place where you will attach the wings and tail, then stick them on with a dab of chocolate.

8

STEP 8
~

Make the hen's feet by pinching ee pointed sausages of red marzipan together. Stick them to the base of the sphere.

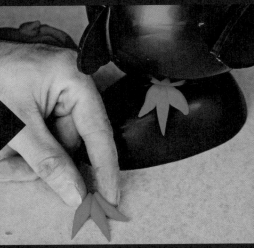

9

STEP 9
~

Make the beak out of yellow marzipan and the eyes in uncolored marzipan with two dots of dark chocolate.

THE END
~≈≈≈≈≈≈≈≈≈~

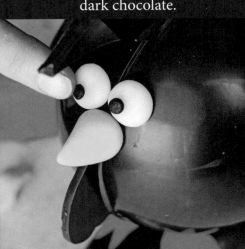

1807 ~ 1825

1761 ~ 1791
A SHOP WITH THE ALLURE OF A FARMHOUSE

1791 ~ 1807
THE FATE OF LE PÈRE DE FAMILLE

*
1807 ~ 1825
A FREE WOMAN
*

1825 ~ 1850
AT THE HEART OF ARTISTIC LIFE

1850 ~ 1895
A NEW ERA OF COOKIES

A

FREE

WOMAN

It is in 1807 that the fate of the store is sealed. Marie-Adélaïde is raising her four children alone after the death of her husband.

She is a woman of character—generous, beautiful, independent, and proud to be able to educate her children while, at the same time, looking after the business she helped to build with her husband. Faithful to their aspirations, she becomes the sole operator of the establishment, a unique situation for a woman at that time. The woman known as "the widow Bridauld" works day and night to build her store. She recruits new apprentices, offers treats in tune with the times, brings in confectionery from other regions of France, and goes traveling herself to taste sweet specialties that are hard to find in Paris so that she may introduce them to customers. Her freedom and independence quickly build her reputation, and the fame of the store soon spreads beyond the neighborhood's boundaries. At the same time, Paris becomes the center of luxury and fashion, and the store wins recognition thanks to the great gastronomic critic of the day, Alexandre-Balthazar-Laurent Grimod de la Reynière. In 1810, the seventh edition of his *Almanach des Gourmands* sings the praises of the widow Bridauld's establishment. Entranced by the young Marie-Adélaïde, the critic devotes a full page to her—a unique honor—and extols her shop as "an establishment worthy of the attention of consumers . . . audacious, delicious, and perfectly run . . . by the amiable and highly interesting Madame Bridauld." À la Mère de Famille undergoes a glorious boom and officially establishes itself as a landmark of Parisian gastronomy.

It is during the Consulate and then the First Empire that Parisians, coming out of the French Revolution, rediscover everyday pleasures, particularly gastronomic ones. This movement leaves us with the name of de la Reynière, founder of the gastronomic clubs of the time and creator of the culinary guide *Almanach des Gourmands*, which aims to steer Parisians towards the best culinary stores of the capital.

LADYFINGERS

MAKES ABOUT **20** LADYFINGERS
PREPARATION TIME **15** MINUTES
COOKING TIME **10** MINUTES

eggs, separated 4
granulated sugar..½ cup
all-purpose flour ....½ cup
confectioners' sugar ....for dusting

MAKING THE BATTER

In a clean dry bowl, whisk the egg whites until foamy, then gradually add the granulated sugar, whisking constantly. Using a spatula, gently fold in the egg yolks, then sift in the flour, being careful to fold it in gently.

BAKING

Preheat the oven to 325°F. Line a baking sheet with parchment paper. Using a pastry bag fitted with a ½-inch tip, form the ladyfingers on the prepared baking sheet. Dust them with confectioners' sugar and bake for 8 to 10 minutes until they are a lovely golden color. Remove from the oven and allow to cool. (Store the ladyfingers in an airtight container away from moisture for up to 1 week.)

HAZELNUT SLAB

MAKES 1 LB

PREPARATION TIME 15 MINUTES
REFRIGERATION TIME 20 MINUTES

1½ cups hazelnuts
7 oz good-quality dark, milk, or white chocolate (preferably couverture)

PREPARING THE HAZELNUTS AND CHOCOLATE
Preheat the oven to 325°F. Place the hazelnuts on a baking sheet and toast for 10 minutes, until golden and fragrant. Remove from the oven (leave the oven on), allow to cool, then rub the nuts in a clean dish towel to remove the skins. Set aside. Temper the chocolate (see page 46). Return the skinned, toasted hazelnuts to the baking sheet and warm in the oven for 3 minutes, until the nuts are about 160°F. Combine the hazelnuts with the chocolate. Pour the mixture onto a rimmed baking sheet lined with parchment paper, forming a layer about ⅜ inch thick.

REFRIGERATION
Place the hazelnut slab in the refrigerator for 20 minutes until set. Turn it out of the baking sheet and break it up with a hammer. (The slab can be stored for up to 1 month in a cool place and away from moisture.)

 Is all we need to achieve pleasure some chocolate, hazelnuts, and a few bangs of a hammer?

NOUGATINE
AND PRALINE PODS

MAKES ABOUT 25 PODS

PREPARATION TIME 1 HOUR
REFRIGERATION TIME 1 HOUR

2 oz good-quality milk chocolate, chopped
¾ cup praline paste (page 48), made with hazelnuts
1 recipe almond–pistachio nougatine (page 138), cut into
about fifty ½-by-1-inch rectangles
Ground almonds, for decorating
Green food coloring, for decorating
White chocolate, for decorating

MAKING THE PRALINE
Melt the milk chocolate in a double boiler. Add the praline paste and stir to combine. Refrigerate the mixture for about 2 hours, stirring it from time to time, until it becomes a thick paste. Scoop the mixture into a piping bag fitted with a ½-inch plain tip. Pipe a line of chocolate-praline paste onto one side of each rectangle of nougatine, then put two rectangles together, forming a chocolate-praline sandwich. Repeat until all rectangles have been used. Refrigerate for 1 hour to set.

FOR DECORATING
Combine the ground almonds with a few drops of green food coloring in a small bowl. Temper the white chocolate (see page 46). Using a fork, dip each nougatine pod in the tempered white chocolate, coating all sides, then roll it in the ground almonds. Tap gently to remove excess coating. Refrigerate for 1 hour to set. (Store the nougatine and praline pods in the refrigerator in an airtight container for up to 1 month.)

BIARRITZ WAVES

MAKES ABOUT 1½ LBS

PREPARATION TIME 20 MINUTES
RESTING TIME 2 HOURS

1½ cups mixed nuts and dried fruit, such as raw almonds, pine nuts,
pistachios, candied orange peel (page 102), and raisins
1 lb good-quality dark, milk, or white chocolate (preferably couverture)

PREPARING THE FRUIT, NUTS, AND CHOCOLATE

Preheat the oven to 325°F. Place the nuts on a baking sheet and toast in the oven
for 10 minutes. Remove from the oven and allow to cool. Temper the chocolate
(see page 46). Spread the chocolate in a thin layer on an acetate sheet to make
a rectangle about ¼ inch thick. Scatter the nuts and dried fruit over the top of
the chocolate.

MAKING THE WAVES

When the chocolate starts to set, lay the acetate sheet over two rolling pins
so that it makes a wavy shape. Allow to set completely, about 2 hours at 65°F.
Carefully remove the sheet of acetate from the chocolate. (Store in an airtight
container for up to 1 month.)

 *The waves of Biarritz are well known to surfers. But these Biarritz waves,
well known to incorrigible gourmands, carry a crunchy tide of fruit and
nuts in their chocolaty crests and troughs.*

CROQUE-TVS

MAKES ABOUT 20 PIECES

PREPARATION TIME 15 MINUTES

MILK CHOCOLATE AND COFFEE
7 oz milk chocolate, chopped
1½ tsp espresso powder

DARK CHOCOLATE AND COCOA NIBS
7 oz dark chocolate (70% cocoa), chopped
2 tbsp cocoa nibs

DARK CHOCOLATE AND ALMONDS
7 oz dark chocolate (70% cocoa), chopped
6 tbsp chopped roasted almonds

WHITE CHOCOLATE AND PISTACHIOS
7 oz white chocolate, chopped
6 tbsp chopped pistachios

MILK CHOCOLATE AND COFFEE
Temper the chocolate (see page 46). Add the espresso powder to the chocolate and stir to combine. Place dollops of tempered chocolate on a sheet of parchment paper and spread them out to make a *langue de chat* (cat's tongue) shape.

DARK CHOCOLATE AND ALMONDS
Temper the chocolate (see page 46). After making the chocolate "tongues," scatter them with chopped almonds.

DARK CHOCOLATE AND COCOA NIBS
Temper the chocolate (see page 46). After making the chocolate "tongues," scatter them with cocoa nibs.

WHITE CHOCOLATE AND PISTACHIOS
Temper the chocolate (see page 46). After making the chocolate "tongues," scatter them with chopped pistachio nuts.

Allow to cool and carefully detach from the sheet. (Store in an airtight container away from moisture for up to 1 month.)

Use couverture chocolate (see page 8) for this recipe— it is easier to work with and gives a better result. If unavailable, it's best to use only dark chocolate with a high percentage of cocoa.

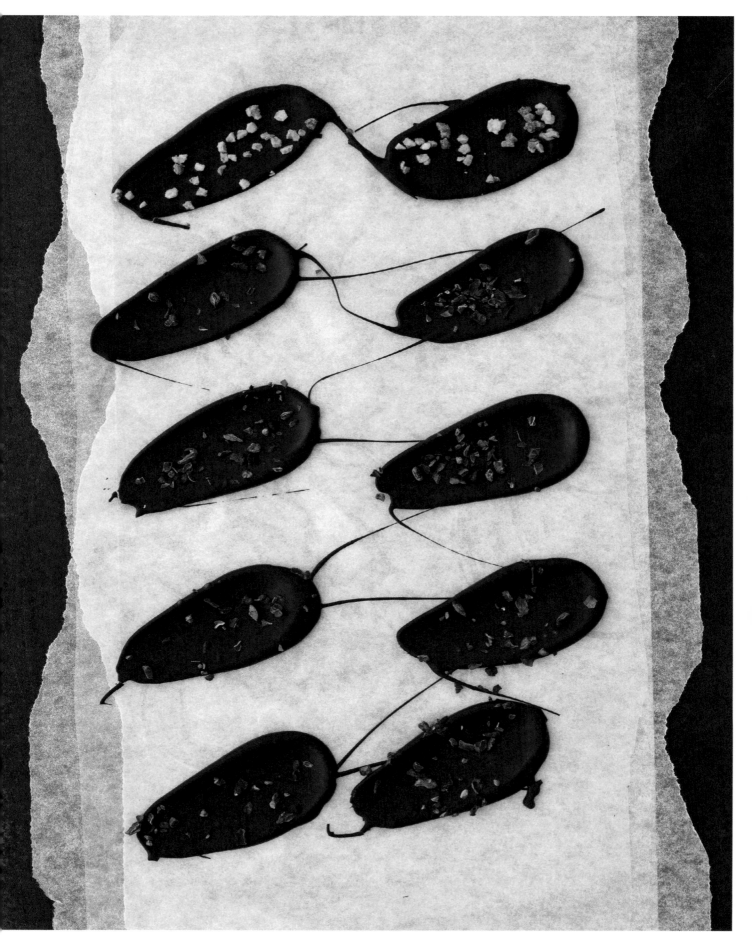

CUSTOMER PORTRAITS:
STÉPHANE MANGIN

OCCUPATION . . . . Antiques seller
NEIGHBORHOOD . . . . Drouot
STORES VISITED . . . . . Rue du Faubourg–Montmartre and
Rue du Cherche–Midi

FIRST VISIT . . . . I've always come here
FREQUENCY OF VISITS . . . . .Once a month
FAVORITE CHOCOLATE . . . . Dark

1
WHEN DO YOU VISIT THE STORE?
Late morning for a pick-me-up before my daily visit to the Hôtel Drouot. It doesn't really matter what season it is, but I never miss the Christmas and Easter window displays.

2
WHAT IS YOUR GREATEST INDULGENCE?
Roaming the aisles, with the eyes before the taste buds—like the torment of Tantalus.

3
YOUR GUILTY PLEASURE?
Centenario rum.

4
WHAT WAS YOUR CHILDHOOD TREAT?
Treets candies.

5
WHAT KIND OF TREATS DO YOU LIKE TO SHARE?
A chocolate *religieuse*—as long as I get the hat.

6
WHAT DO YOU THINK IS THE MOST ROMANTIC TREAT?
Sharing those wonderful pink and bluish marshmallows with one's soul mate on the highest branch of the tallest tree.

7
THE MOST AMUSING TREAT?
Alfred! The irresistible figurine from Christmas 2009.

8
HAVE YOU EVER BEEN INSPIRED BY A SWEET?
I fell in love with a chocolate Yoruba mask from À La Mère de Famille, which I spontaneously included in my collection of African art. I kept it in the refrigerator for a year and a half without having the nerve to attack it. Not bad!

9
DESCRIBE A PERFECT MOMENT TIED TO A TREAT FROM À LA MÈRE DE FAMILLE.
The day I finally decided to shatter the mask in question, and eat it (alone). It was as good as it was beautiful.

10
IF LA MÈRE WERE TO GIVE YOU A PRESENT, WHAT WOULD YOU LIKE IT TO BE?
Up to her! I have complete trust! The orange packaging and its famous ribbon always herald sweet pleasures.

11
WHAT DOES À LA MÈRE DE FAMILLE REPRESENT FOR YOU?
The devil! It's good that they exist.

12
WHAT DO YOU THINK SHOULD BE THE MOTTO OF À LA MÈRE DE FAMILLE?
"In search of lost time."

13
WHAT IS THE SECRET TO ITS ENDURING SUCCESS?
Humor.

14
WHAT DOES THE STORE'S HISTORY EVOKE FOR YOU?
Respect and tenderness.

15
WHY DO YOU LOVE À LA MÈRE DE FAMILLE?
It goes without saying.

ROCHERS

PREPARATION TIME 40 MINUTES
RESTING TIME OVERNIGHT + 1¼ HOURS

PRALINE-ALMOND ROCHERS

3 oz good-quality milk chocolate, chopped
1 cup plus 1 tbsp praline paste (page 48)
8 oz dark chocolate, chopped
½ cup chopped roasted almonds

PREPARING THE PRALINE
In a double boiler, melt the milk chocolate and stir in the praline paste. Cover and set aside overnight at 65°F. Shape into balls weighing about 1½ oz each and allow them to firm up in the refrigerator for 15 minutes.

MAKING THE ROCHERS
Temper the dark chocolate (see page 48) and stir in the chopped almonds. Roll each ball in the chocolate until coated. Place the rochers on a baking sheet lined with parchment paper. Allow to set in the refrigerator for 1 hour. (Store away from moisture in an airtight container for up to 1 month.)

PRALINE-PISTACHIO ROCHERS

3 oz good-quality milk chocolate, chopped
10 oz praline paste (page 48)
1 oz pistachio paste (page 160)
8 oz dark chocolate, chopped
½ cup chopped pistachios

PREPARING THE PRALINE
In a double boiler, melt the milk chocolate and stir in the praline and pistachio pastes. Cover and set aside overnight at 65°F. Shape into balls weighing about 1½ oz each and allow them to firm up in the refrigerator for 15 minutes.

MAKING THE ROCHERS
Temper the dark chocolate (see page 48) and stir in 2 tbsp of the chopped pistachios. Roll each ball in the chocolate until coated. Place the rochers on a baking sheet lined with parchment paper and scatter over the remaining pistachios. Allow to set in the refrigerator for 1 hour. (Store away from moisture in an airtight container for up to 1 month.)

PRALINE-SESAME ROCHERS

3 oz good-quality milk chocolate, chopped
10 oz praline paste (page 48)
1 oz black sesame paste
8 oz dark chocolate, chopped
¼ cup toasted sesame seeds

PREPARING THE PRALINE
In a double boiler, melt the milk chocolate and stir in the praline and sesame pastes. Cover and set aside overnight at 65°F. Shape into balls weighing about 1½ oz each and allow them to firm up in the refrigerator for 15 minutes.

MAKING THE ROCHERS
Temper the dark chocolate (see page 48) and stir in 2 tbsp of the sesame seeds. Roll each ball in the chocolate until coated. Place the rochers on a baking sheet lined with parchment paper and scatter over the remaining sesame seeds. Allow to set in the refrigerator for 1 hour. (Store away from moisture in an airtight container for up to 1 month.)

These rochers are a real stumbling block for those who were hoping to resist succumbing to a chocolate temptation.

BIARRITZ ROCHERS

MAKES 20 PIECES

PREPARATION TIME 30 MINUTES
REFRIGERATION TIME 15 MINUTES

1¼ cups slivered almonds
3½ oz good-quality dark or milk chocolate, chopped
1½ oz candied orange peel (page 102), diced

Preheat the oven to 325°F. Place the slivered almonds on a baking sheet and toast in the oven for about 6 minutes, until golden. Remove from the oven and allow to cool. Temper the chocolate (see page 46). Add the almonds and diced orange peel and mix well. Using a spoon, make small mounds of the mixture on a baking sheet lined with parchment paper. Refrigerate for 15 minutes to set before detaching the rochers from the paper. (Store for up to 1 month in an airtight container away from moisture.)

PALET OR

PREPARATION TIME 55 MINUTES
RESTING TIME OVERNIGHT + 2 HOURS

1½ lbs dark chocolate (70% cocoa)
1 vanilla bean, split lengthwise
1 cup whipping cream
3 tbsp unsalted butter, softened
Gold leaf, for garnish

MAKING THE GANACHE

Chop 7 oz of the chocolate and place in a mixing bowl. Scrape the seeds from the vanilla bean into a medium saucepan. Pour in the cream, set over medium heat, and bring to just under a boil. Strain the hot cream into the bowl with the chocolate and stir gently with a spatula to make a smooth ganache. When it is lukewarm (85°F), stir in the softened butter. Cover the ganache with plastic wrap and allow it to set overnight at room temperature.

FORMING THE CHOCOLATES

Scoop the ganache into a piping bag fitted with a small plain tip. Pipe small balls of ganache (about ½ inch each) onto an acetate sheet. Cover with a second acetate sheet and gently flatten the balls into pucks about ⅛ inch thick. Let set for at least 2 hours at 65°F.

COATING

Temper the remaining chocolate (see page 46). Remove the acetate sheet on top of the flattened chocolates. Using a spatula or pastry brush, cover the top of each with a thin coating of tempered chocolate. Allow the coating to set, then turn the chocolates over and coat the second sides. Finish by placing a small piece of gold leaf on each.

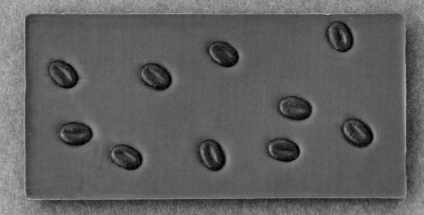

A LA MÈRE DE FAMILLE
Maison fondée en 1761
MAGASIN SPÉCIAL DE DESSERTS D'HIVER
G. LECŒUR
35, Faubourg Montmartre et 1 Rue de Provence
Téléphone : Gutenberg 25-46

A LA MÈRE DE FAMILLE
Maison fondée en 1761
MAGASIN SPÉCIAL DE DESSERTS D'HIVER

G. LECŒUR
35, Faubourg Montmartre et 1, Rue de Provence
Téléphone : Gutenberg 25-48

CHOCOLATE BARS

PREPARATION TIME 15 MINUTES
REFRIGERATION TIME 20 MINUTES

MENDIANT

¼ cup hazelnuts
¼ cup almonds
10½ oz good-quality dark chocolate
(preferably couverture)
1 tbsp pistachios
2 tbsp raisins
2 tbsp diced candied orange peel (page 102)

Preheat the oven to 325°F. Place the hazelnuts and almonds on a baking sheet and toast for 10 minutes. Allow to cool. Temper the chocolate (see page 46) and pour it into three 3½-oz chocolate-bar molds. Scatter the fruit and nuts on top. Refrigerate for 20 minutes before unmolding.

CANDIED ORANGE PEEL

1½ cups diced candied orange peel
(page 102)
A splash of Grand Marnier
10½ oz good-quality dark chocolate
(preferably couverture)

Combine the candied peel with the Grand Marnier in a bowl and break up any clumps. Temper the chocolate (see page 46) and pour it into three 3½-oz chocolate-bar molds. Scatter the soaked peel on top. Refrigerate for 20 minutes before unmolding.

CRUNCH

10½ oz good-quality dark chocolate
(preferably couverture)
1½ tbsp *perles croustillantes* (crunchy
chocolate pearls) or puffed rice

Temper the chocolate (see page 46) and pour it into three 3½-oz chocolate-bar molds. Scatter the *perles croustillantes* on top. Refrigerate for 20 minutes before unmolding.

ALMONDS

10½ oz good-quality dark chocolate
(preferably couverture)
⅓ cup unblanched almonds

Preheat the oven to 325°C. Place the almonds on a baking sheet and toast for 10 minutes. Allow to cool, then roughly chop. Temper the chocolate (see page 46) and pour it into three 3½-oz chocolate-bar molds. Scatter the almonds on top. Refrigerate for 20 minutes before unmolding.

STORAGE: *The chocolate bars can be stored in an airtight container in a cool, dry place for up to 1 month.*

FOLIES DE L'ÉCUREUIL

MAKES ABOUT 5 CUPS

PREPARATION TIME 1½ HOURS

FOR THE CARAMELIZED NUTS
1½ cups hazelnuts
1½ cups unblanched almonds
¾ cup sugar
⅓ cup water

FOR COATING
5 oz dark chocolate (70% cocoa)
Unsweetened cocoa powder

CARAMELIZING THE NUTS

Preheat the oven to 350°F. Place the hazelnuts and almonds on a baking sheet and toast for 10 minutes. Remove from the oven and allow to cool completely. Put the sugar and water in a large saucepan, set over medium-low heat, and cook until the mixture registers about 245°F on a candy thermometer. Add the almonds and hazelnuts, turn down the heat to low, and stir with a wooden spoon. The syrup will coat the nuts, then become gritty as it crystallizes around them. Continue to mix until the sugar starts to caramelize, but before it completely melts. Tip the nuts out onto a baking sheet and allow them to cool completely. Make sure each nut is separated and dries individually.

COATING THE NUTS

Place the caramelized almonds and hazelnuts in a large mixing bowl. Temper the chocolate (see page 46). Pour some of the tempered chocolate over the nuts in a thin stream, mixing with a spatula at the same time. Wait for the chocolate to start to harden before adding more. Keep stirring until the chocolate sets. To finish, lightly dust the nuts with cocoa and shake in a strainer to remove any excess.

TOUCANS

MAKES ABOUT 50 PIECES

PREPARATION TIME 40 MINUTES
RESTING TIME 30 + 15 MINUTES

3 oz good-quality milk chocolate
1 cup plus 1 tbsp praline paste (page 48)
1 oz *crêpes dentelles* or other crisp, sweet cookies, crumbled
¼ cup roasted almonds, chopped
10 oz dark chocolate (70% cocoa), chopped
Unsweetened cocoa powder, for coating

PREPARING THE CHOCOLATE

In a double boiler, melt the milk chocolate and stir in the praline paste, followed by the crumbled cookies and the chopped almonds. Set aside in a cool place, stirring from time to time until thickened. Fit a piping bag with a ½-inch plain tip and fill the bag with the chocolate mixture. Pipe the mixture onto a baking sheet lined with parchment paper, forming it into long lengths ½ inch in diameter and as even in thickness as possible. Refrigerate for 10 minutes to set, then cut into 1½-inch logs.

FINISHING

Temper the dark chocolate (see page 46). Dip the logs in the tempered chocolate, roll them in cocoa powder, and shake gently in a strainer to remove any excess. (Store away from moisture in an airtight container at 65°F for up to 1 month.)

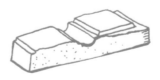

 VARIATION: *Try making these toucans using chopped macadamia nuts instead of almonds, and enjoy the difference!*

A LA MÈRE DE FAMILLE
35, Rue du Faubourg-Montmartre

NÉNUPHAR. — Impuissance, Froideur

À LA MÈRE DE FAMILLE
Mon FONDÉE EN 1761
CONFISERIE ET DESSERTS

MAISON FOND
E FAMILLE
biscuits
LEFÈVRE-UTILE
biscuits
LEFÈVRE-UTILE
35
VINS FINS D
MAGASIN SPÉCIAL du DESS
FRUITS SECS pour COMPO
SECS
FRUITS
SPECIALITE
DE
MIEL
MÉRE DE F

TRUFFLES

MAKES ABOUT 50 PIECES

PREPARATION TIME 40 MINUTES
RESTING TIME 24 HOURS

7 oz dark chocolate (70% cocoa)
1¼ cups heavy cream
1½ tbsp unsalted butter, softened
Unsweetened cocoa powder, for coating

MAKING THE GANACHE
Chop the chocolate and place in a large mixing bowl. Heat the cream in a small saucepan over medium-low heat to just under a boil, then pour it over the chocolate. Using a spatula, gently stir to combine and emulsify the ganache—be careful not to incorporate any air. Add the butter and stir to combine. Cover and set aside for 24 hours at 65°F to allow the ganache to set.

FORMING THE TRUFFLES
Shape the ganache into walnut-size balls. Roll in cocoa powder to coat and shake gently in a strainer to remove any excess. (Store in an airtight container at 65°F for up to 5 days.)

FANCY TRUFFLES

MAKES ABOUT 50 PIECES

PREPARATION TIME 40 MINUTES
RESTING TIME 24 HOURS

COFFEE

1 cup whipping cream
2 tsp crushed coffee beans
1 lb dark chocolate (70% cocoa), chopped
1 tbsp unsalted butter, softened
Unsweetened cocoa powder, for coating

Heat the cream in a small saucepan and warm over medium heat to just under a boil. Remove from the heat, add the coffee beans, and leave to infuse for 5 minutes. Place 10 oz of the chocolate in a medium bowl. Gently reheat the cream and pour it through a strainer over the chocolate. Using a spatula, stir gently to combine and emulsify the ganache, being careful not to incorporate any air. Add the butter and fold to combine. Cover and set aside for 24 hours at 65°F.

Shape the ganache into walnut-size balls and set on a baking sheet lined with parchment paper. Temper the remaining chocolate (see page 46). Dip each ball in the tempered chocolate to coat, roll in cocoa powder, and shake gently in a strainer to remove any excess.

CARAMEL

5 oz good-quality milk chocolate, chopped
⅓ cup sugar
¾ cup whipping cream, warmed
A pinch of salt
2 tbsp unsalted butter, softened
10 oz dark chocolate (70% cocoa), chopped
Unsweetened cocoa powder, for coating

Place the milk chocolate in a medium bowl. Put the sugar in a medium saucepan and make dry caramel, following the instructions on page 8. Stir the cream into the caramel, then add the salt. Pour the warm caramel over the milk chocolate. Using a spatula, stir gently to combine and emulsify the ganache, being careful not to incorporate any air. Add the butter and fold to combine. Cover and set aside for 24 hours at 65°F.

Shape the ganache into walnut-size balls and set on a baking sheet lined with parchment paper. Temper the dark chocolate (see page 46). Dip each ball in the tempered chocolate to coat, roll in cocoa powder, and shake gently in a strainer to remove any excess.

MILK CHOCOLATE

9 oz good-quality milk chocolate, chopped
½ cup plus 2 tbsp whipping cream
2 tbsp unsalted butter, softened
3.5 oz crumbled flaky butter cookies, such as *crêpes dentelles*, for coating

Place the milk chocolate in a medium bowl. Heat the cream in a small saucepan over medium heat to just under a boil, then pour it over the milk chocolate. Using a spatula, stir gently to combine and emulsify the ganache, being careful not to incorporate any air. Add the butter and fold to combine. Cover and set aside for 24 hours at 65°F.

Shape the ganache into walnut-size balls and set on a baking sheet lined with parchment paper. Roll the balls in the crumbled cookies, then shake to remove any excess.

 STORAGE: *Store the truffles in an airtight container for up to 10 days.*

CHOCOLATE-MENDIANT
LOLLIPOPS

MAKES 10 LOLLIPOPS

PREPARATION TIME 20 MINUTES
RESTING TIME 30 MINUTES

3½ oz dark chocolate (70% cocoa)
Mixed dried fruit, such apples, pears, figs, and raisins, chopped
Chopped pistachios

PREPARING THE TEMPLATES AND CHOCOLATE
On two or three sheets of paper, draw ten 2¾-inch circles. Cover each sheet of paper with a sheet of acetate. Temper the chocolate (see page 46). Fit a piping bag with a small plain tip and fill the bag with the chocolate.

FORMING THE LOLLIPOPS
Place a lollipop stick on each circle with one end of the stick at the very center of the circle. Using the circles as a guide, pipe overlapping lines of chocolate in swirls onto the acetate sheets and on the sticks, making sure you stay inside the lines. Scatter dried fruit and pistachios on the swirls of chocolate. Pipe more lines of chocolate on top of the fruit and nuts so they are well attached. Allow to set for 30 minutes at 65°F before carefully detaching the lollipops from the acetate.

VARIATION: *This sweet delight is a classic combination of chocolate and dried fruit, but in the form of a pretty lollipop. To change things up a bit, look for dried fruits that are a bit out of the ordinary, such as pineapple and mango. Having said that, these are delicious made with fat golden raisins!*

1825 ~ 1850

1761 ~ 1791	1791 ~ 1807	1807 ~ 1825	1825 ~ 1850 *	1850 ~ 1895
A SHOP WITH THE ALLURE OF A FARMHOUSE	THE FATE OF LE PÈRE DE FAMILLE	A FREE WOMAN	AT THE HEART OF ARTISTIC LIFE *	A NEW ERA OF COOKIES

AT THE HEART OF ARTISTIC LIFE

During the first half of the nineteenth century, artists and the bourgeoisie replace the aristocracy in Paris's 9th arrondissement. Painters, writers, and musicians become habitués of the Rue du Faubourg-Montmartre and its famous fine food boutique. Berlioz, Chopin, and George Sand move into the neighborhood and, a few steps away, on Rue de la Grange Batelière, Hugo, Sainte-Beuve, Lamartine, and Musset have their weekly meetings. The widow Bridauld's store is the only one in the neighborhood to offer such a selection of delicacies, and paying her a visit becomes more than a fashion—it's a way of life. Dinners and other engagements are accompanied by sweetmeats from À la Mère de Famille; children press their noses to the window; and people come from far and wide to admire the work of Marie-Adélaïde Bridauld. Ferdinand, the eldest son, takes his first steps in his mother's food shop.

Throughout his childhood, he watches her receive customers, advise them, and nurture her establishment. He grows up in the neighborhood, where he meets Joséphine, the granddaughter of the founder of the store. After their marriage, the family of the shop's proprietors and that of its managers are reunited. Under the direction of Joséphine and Ferdinand, À la Mère de Famille continues to prosper, a symbol of their relationship. Meanwhile, the neighborhood becomes one of the most fashionable in Paris.

When the tensions between France and England prevent raw materials from France's colonies (including cane sugar) from reaching the mainland, Napoleon I decides to support research into a substitute product. The first industrial extraction of beet sugar, in 1812, paves the way for modern confectionery. In the following few years, numerous processing plants are created, enabling the democratization and growth of the confectionery domain. Fine food stores start to sell their own preserves and invent more elaborate sweets thanks to the creation of candy sugar in 1830.

1895 ~ 1920
A CHILDHOOD DREAM COME TRUE

1920 ~ 1950
THE SOUL OF THE NEIGHBORHOOD

1950 ~ 1985
ALBERT AND SUZANNE

1985 ~ 2000
A TIME FOR CHOCOLATE

2000 ~
HISTORY IN THE MAKING

NONETTES

MAKES **20** CAKES
PREPARATION TIME **15** MINUTES
BAKING TIME **17** MINUTES

BATTER AND FILLING

orange marmalade (page 202) .... 1 cup
all-purpose flour .... 2¼ cups
baking powder.. 1 tbsp
granulated sugar .... ¾ cup
milk .... ¾ cup
honey .... ½ cup
unsalted butter, softened.. 5½ tsp

ICING

water .... 1½ tbsp
confectioners' sugar .... ½ cup

Making the batter and filling

If the marmalade is runny, cook it in a small saucepan over medium heat for a few minutes until thick, then let cool. In a large mixing bowl, whisk together the flour, baking powder, and granulated sugar. In a medium saucepan over medium heat, heat the milk and honey until lukewarm. Pour the milk and honey over the dry ingredients, stir well, then add the butter and stir until just combined.

BAKING

Preheat the oven to 325°F. Lightly grease twenty 2-inch cake rings or similar baking molds. Place the rings on a baking sheet lined with parchment paper. Divide the batter evenly among the prepared rings, then spoon 1½ tsp of the marmalade on to each. Bake for 15 minutes, or until golden—the marmalade will sink inside the cakes during baking.

ICING

While the cakes are baking, in a small bowl, whisk together the water and confectioners' sugar to make a runny icing. When the cakes are golden, remove them from the oven, brush each with icing, and return to the oven for 2 minutes. Allow to cool on a wire rack for at least 20 minutes before removing the rings. Store in an airtight container for up to 3 days.

CHOCOLATE-DIPPED
ORANGE PEEL

MAKES ABOUT 1 LB

PREPARATION TIME 30 MINUTES
CANDYING TIME 40 MINUTES OVER 5 DAYS

FOR THE CANDIED ORANGE PEEL
5 oranges
Water
Salt
2⅓ cups sugar

FOR DIPPING
10½ oz dark chocolate (70% cocoa)

MAKING THE CANDIED ORANGE PEEL
Wash the oranges and remove the peel with a sharp vegetable peeler, avoiding any white pith. Put the orange peel in a saucepan with 4 cups water and a pinch of salt. Bring to a boil over high heat and boil for 5 minutes. Drain. Repeat this process one more time.

Put 1 cup of the sugar and 1⅔ cups water in a clean saucepan and bring to a boil, stirring until the sugar dissolves. Add the blanched orange peel to the boiling syrup, immediately remove from the heat, cover the pan, and set aside overnight at room temperature.

The next day, drain the peel, reserving the syrup. Add ⅓ cup of the remaining sugar to the reserved syrup, bring to a boil, and return the peel to the syrup. Remove from the heat, cover, and set aside overnight at room temperature. Repeat this process three more times, over three nights, adding ⅓ cup sugar each time. Once the peel is candied, let drain at room temperature for 1 day, then cut into thin slivers. (The peel can be stored in an airtight container for up to 1 month.)

DIPPING
Temper the dark chocolate (see page 46). Using a fork, dip each strip of candied orange peel in the chocolate, then lay it on an acetate sheet. Refrigerate the chocolate-dipped strips for 10 minutes before detaching from the sheet. (Store in a cool place away from moisture for up to 1 month.)

 CHEF'S TIP: *For this recipe, it's best to use organic oranges if you can find them. (If using conventional ones, scrub them thoroughly.) Try grapefruits instead of oranges for an equally inspiring result!*

CHOCOLATE LOLLIPOPS FOR HOT MILK

MAKES 10 LOLLIPOPS

PREPARATION TIME 10 MINUTES

MILK CHOCOLATE-HAZELNUT

7 oz good-quality milk chocolate
1½ tbsp praline paste (page 48), made with hazelnuts

MAKING THE LOLLIPOPS
Temper the milk chocolate (see page 46). Add the praline paste and stir to combine. Divide evenly among ten silicone mini-muffin molds. Insert a wooden spoon into each mold and refrigerate for 15 minutes, or until set, before removing from the molds. (Store in an airtight container for up to 1 week.)

SERVING
Pour ¾ cup of hot milk into a cup. Add the chocolate lollipop and stir with the wooden spoon until the chocolate has completely melted.

DARK CHOCOLATE-ORANGE

7 oz dark chocolate (70% cocoa)
4 drops orange oil

MAKING THE LOLLIPOPS
Temper the dark chocolate (see page 46). Add the orange oil and stir to combine. Divide evenly among ten silicone mini-muffin molds. Insert a wooden spoon into each mold and refrigerate for 15 minutes, or until set, before removing from the molds. (Store in an airtight container for up to 1 week.)

SERVING
Pour ¾ cup of hot milk into a cup. Add the chocolate lollipop and stir with the wooden spoon until the chocolate has completely melted.

WHITE CHOCOLATE-COCONUT

7 oz good-quality white chocolate
3 tbsp unsweetened shredded coconut

MAKING THE LOLLIPOPS
Temper the white chocolate (see page 46). Add the coconut and stir to combine. Divide evenly among ten silicone mini-muffin molds. Insert a wooden spoon into each mold and refrigerate for 15 minutes, or until set, before removing from the molds. (Store in an airtight container for up to 1 week.)

SERVING
Pour ¾ cup of hot milk into a cup. Add the chocolate lollipop and stir with the wooden spoon until the chocolate has completely melted.

3

**IT'S A DREAM COME TRUE!
YOU CAN MAKE YOUR OWN
CANDY** in a single afternoon, transforming
your kitchen into a sugar workshop, creating treats
for yourself and, if there are children around you,
ensuring your lasting and unwavering popularity
among them. Marshmallows, hard candies, and
nougats: there's a whole host of old-fashioned
sweets captured in these pages. And, oh, miracle
of miracles! There is even—*shhhhh*—the recipe for
our marshmallow teddy bears!

CANDYMAKING

BLACK CURRANT MARSHMALLOW

MAKES ABOUT 50 SMALL MARSHMALLOWS

PREPARATION TIME 25 MINUTES
RESTING TIME 3 HOURS

½ oz gelatin sheets
1¼ cups granulated sugar
¼ cup black currant purée
2½ tbsp mild honey
1½ tbsp water

3 egg whites
powdered violet food coloring (optional)
⅔ cup confectioners' sugar
⅔ cup potato starch

MAKING THE MARSHMALLOW

Place the gelatin in cold water and soak for 5 minutes, then drain and set aside. In a medium saucepan, combine the granulated sugar, purée, honey, and water and cook over medium-high heat, stirring occasionally, until the mixture registers 235°F on a candy thermometer. Meanwhile, in the clean, dry bowl of a stand mixer, whip the egg whites with the whisk attachment on low speed. Gently fold in the hot black currant mixture, then the softened gelatin. Continue to whip the mixture on high speed until it thickens and is warm to the touch. Add the food coloring and stir to combine.

CUTTING INTO CUBES

Combine the confectioners' sugar and potato starch in a small bowl. When the marshmallow mixture has cooled to about 105°F, sprinkle a clean work surface with two-thirds of the starch mixture. Turn the marshmallow out onto the work surface and spread it into a rectangle about 1 inch thick. Flip the rectangle to coat both sides with the starch mixture. Let the marshmallow cool at room temperature for 3 hours before cutting into 1¼-inch cubes. Toss the cubes of marshmallow with the remaining starch mixture to prevent them from sticking together.

 VARIATION: *To make plain marshmallow, replace the black currant pulp with 5 tbsp of water and omit the food coloring. To make strawberry marshmallow, replace the black currant pulp with ¼ cup of strawberry pulp.*

MARSHMALLOW

{ MADE STEP-BY-STEP }

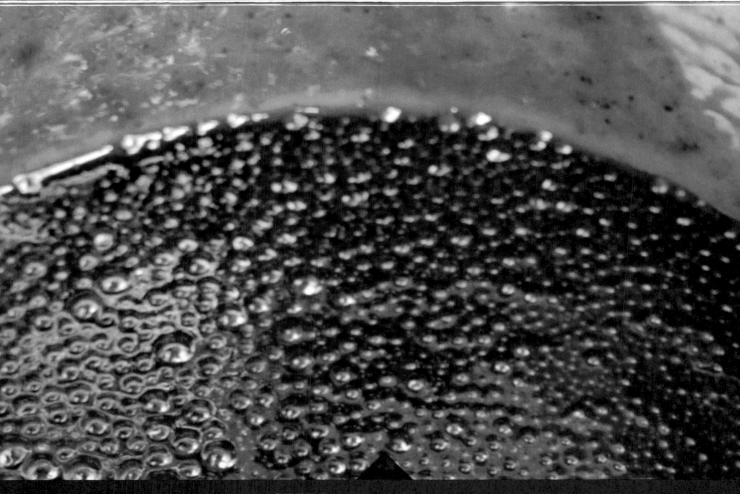

STEP 2

~

Cook the sugar, black currant purée,
honey, and water until the mixture
registers 235°F on a candy thermometer.

2

STEP 1

~

Soak the gelatin in cold water for 5 minutes, then drain.

STEP 3

~

Gently incorporate the black currant mixture into the beaten egg whites, then add the softened gelatin. Whip the mixture on high speed—the marshmallow will expand, then cool. Now add the coloring.

STEP 4

~

When the mixture has cooled to 105°F, turn it out onto a clean work surface sprinkled with a mixture of confectioners' sugar and potato starch, then cut into cubes.

THE END

MARSHMALLOWS FOR ALL TASTES

MAKES ABOUT 50 SMALL MARSHMALLOWS

PREPARATION TIME 25 MINUTES
RESTING TIME 3 HOURS

LIME MARSHMALLOW

½ oz gelatin sheets
¼ cup lime juice
2 tbsp water
2½ tbsp mild honey
1⅓ cups granulated sugar
3 egg whites
1 pinch of powdered green food coloring (optional)
1 pinch of powdered yellow food coloring (optional)
⅔ cup confectioners' sugar
⅔ cup potato starch

RASPBERRY MARSHMALLOW

½ oz gelatin sheets
⅓ cup raspberry purée
1½ tbsp water
2½ tbsp mild honey
1⅓ cups granulated sugar
3 egg whites
1 pinch of powdered red food coloring (optional)
⅔ cup confectioners' sugar
⅔ cup potato starch

PASSION FRUIT MARSHMALLOW

½ oz gelatin sheets
¼ cup strained passion fruit purée
1½ tbsp water
2½ tbsp mild honey
1⅓ cups granulated sugar
3 egg whites
1 pinch of powdered yellow food coloring (optional)
⅔ cup confectioners' sugar
⅔ cup potato starch

ROSE MARSHMALLOW

½ oz gelatin sheets
½ cup water
2½ tbsp mild honey
1⅓ cups granulated sugar
3 egg whites
2 tbsp rosewater
1 pinch of powdered pink food coloring (optional)
⅔ cup confectioners' sugar
⅔ cup potato starch

MAKING THE MARSHMALLOW

Follow the instructions on page 108 to make the marshmallow, using the flavorings listed above to make your choice of flavors.

CHOCOLATE MARSHMALLOWS

MAKES ABOUT 50 SMALL MARSHMALLOWS

PREPARATION TIME 25 MINUTES
RESTING TIME 3 HOURS

3½ oz gelatin sheets
2 tbsp water
2½ tbsp mild honey
1⅓ cups sugar
3 tbsp extra-brute cocoa powder
3 egg whites
1 cup unsweetened cocoa powder

MAKING THE MARSHMALLOW

Place the gelatin in cold water and soak for 5 minutes, then drain and set aside. In a medium saucepan, combine the water, honey, sugar, and extra-brute cocoa powder, and cook over medium-high heat, stirring occasionally, until the mixture registers 235°F on a candy thermometer. Meanwhile, in the clean, dry bowl of a stand mixer, whip the egg whites with the whisk attachment on low speed. Gently incorporate the hot sugar syrup, then the softened gelatin. Continue to whip the mixture on high speed until it thickens and is warm to the touch.

CUTTING INTO CUBES

When the marshmallow mixture has cooled to about 105°F, sprinkle a clean work surface with two-thirds of the unsweetened cocoa powder. Turn the marshmallow out onto the work surface and spread into a rectangle about 1 inch thick. Flip the rectangle to coat both sides with cocoa. Let the marshmallow cool at room temperature for 3 hours before cutting into 1¼-inch cubes. Dust the cubes of marshmallow with the remaining cocoa powder to prevent them from sticking together.

MARSHMALLOW TEDDY BEARS

MAKES 30 BEARS

PREPARATION TIME 30 MINUTES
RESTING TIME 2 HOURS

1 recipe plain marshmallow
(see variation, page 108)
10½ oz good-quality milk chocolate

PREPARING THE MOLDS
Temper the chocolate (see page 46). Using a pastry brush, coat thirty 1-inch silicone teddy-bear molds with the tempered chocolate. Place in the refrigerator to harden, about 15 minutes.

FILLING THE MOLDS
Make the plain marshmallow, allow to cool to 80°F, then fill the molds. Refrigerate for 1 hour until the marshmallow is completely cooled.

COATING THE TEDDY BEARS
Reheat the chocolate to using temperature and cover the backs of the teddy bears by applying a final coat of chocolate with a spatula. Let set for 1 hour at 65°F before carefully removing from the molds. (Store in an airtight container for up to 1 month.)

A la Mère de Famille

Serge NEVEU, Chocolatier fabricant

CONFISERIE
DESSERTS

35, Rue du Faubourg Montmartre
et 1, Rue de Provence - PARIS

Téléphone 47 70 83 69

FONDÉE en 1761

FIGUES ROYALES LOCOUM

DE
SMYRNE

DE
SMYRNE

Maison fondée en 1761

A LA MÈRE DE FAMILLE

Serge Neveu règne depuis trois ans sur la plus ancienne
confiserie de Paris, et aussi la plus jolie.

• Massis Bleue : 27, rue Bleue,
9ᵉ. Tél : 48.24.93.36.
• Heratchian : 6, rue Lamartine, 9ᵉ. Tél. 48.78.43.19. C. M.

SALÉ

MAITRES FROMAGERS.
Ils sont tous des artisans pas-
sionnés par leur métier. Affi-
neurs, ils ont à cœur de pro-
poser des fromages au mieux
de leur forme.

CHÈVRES. Cette crèmerie
de quartier aux murs de mar-
bre restés intacts depuis
1900 s'est taillée une belle
réputation. On y croise Al-
phonse Boudard, Jean-Claude
Carrière ou Francis Perrin.
Jean Molard s'est spécialisé
dans le chèvre fermier — no-
tamment du Lyonnais, Loire-
Atlantique, Poitou — et
concocte lui-même des
« curiosités » comme le ca-
membert au calvados
(26,90 F), le boursault au
whisky ou le chèvre raisin-
rhum.

• Molard : 48, rue des Martyrs,
9ᵉ. Tél : 45.26.84.88.

GOUTEUX. Cette fermette
a des allures de campagne
avec son toit de chaume et ses
étagères de bois. Plus de
180 sortes de fromages affinés
par les soins de Henri Voy.
Spécialité : le saint-hubert, un
triple crème moelleux, le vrai
« brin d'amour » corse, un ca-
membert « de Paris » au lait
cru — bien sûr...

...peut-être, qui a œuvré pour le
... gourmand. Depuis 16 ans,
... est l'âme de l'Étoile d'Or.
On y déniche des spécialités
... introuvables ailleurs, comme
... chocolats du Lyonnais
Bernachon, le « Tap de Li-
... » qu'elle va chercher elle-
... même en gare d'Austerlitz, le
... Delicia » de Palomas, la
... oire de Pralus, le Mandarin
... renoblois, etc. La liste serait
... ongue, car Denise Acabo a
... un palais particulièrement
... fin »... Les Japonais, conquis
par le personnage, voulaient
tout acheter en bloc : la dame,
la boutique, la dame dans la
boutique ! Mais pas question,
Denise s'amuse bien trop avec
« ses copains des théâtres d'à
côté » !

cosmopolite, riche en produits
orientaux. Pour les incondi-
tionnels de falafels, loukoums
et autres pâtisseries orienta-
les, deux passages obligés :
Massis Bleue et la célèbre
boutique Heratchian.

• Fouquet : 36, rue Laffitte, 9ᵉ.
Tél : 47.70.85.00.
• A la Mère de Famille : 35,
rue du Faubourg-Montmartre,
9ᵉ. Tél : 47.70.83.69.
• La Bonbonnière de la Tri-
nité : 4, rue Blanche, 9ᵉ. Tél :
48.74.23.38.
• A l'Étoile d'Or : 30, rue Lamartine, 9ᵉ. Tél : 48.74.59.55.

A la MÈRE de FAMILLE

MAISON FONDÉE EN 1761

MAGASIN
SPÉCIAL
DE DESSERTS D'HIVER

GRAND CHOIX
de FRUITS SECS
POUR COMPOTES

Véritable
Cake-Anglais
et Fours Secs
pour le Thé

SERGE NEVEU

35, Faubg Montmartre
et 1, Rue de Provence 1
75009 PARIS

Tél. 47 70 83 69

A la Mère de Famille

CONFISERIE
DESSERTS

35, RUE DU FAUBOURG MONTMARTRE
ET 1, RUE DE PROVENCE PARIS

TÉLÉPHONE : PROVENCE 83-69

C. C. P. PARIS 10.800-06

FONDÉE EN 1761

R. C. SEINE 57 A 16.275

MAISON RECOMMANDÉE SPÉCIALISÉE

Maison Fondée en 1761

R. C. SEINE 57 A 16.279
C. C. P. PARIS 10.800 06

Tél. : 770-83-69

A LA MÈRE DE FAMILLE
CONFISERIE & DESSERTS
VINS FINS · LIQUEURS · CHAMPAGNES

Ancienne maison R. LEGRAND

A. BRETHONNEAU
35, Faubourg Montmartre et 1, Rue de Provence

75009 PARIS, le 15 Mars 1978

Madame Glacier
Gesnes - Montsurs -   Doit

500 g œufs assortis			43	.
3 x 250 Coquillage P.A	x 18.50		55	50
2 paq Croquignoles	x 6.50		13	.
2 x 250 œuf et Moulage Choco	x 21.50		43	.
500 fondants sans sucre			15	.
500 œufs assortis (M: Lebourdais)			43	.
500 Calissons assortis			32	.
500 Choco œufs noirs pref (M: Germaine)			43	.
250 œuf et moulage (Nicole)			21	50
			309	00
	10% -		30	90
			278	10
	Port		8	80
			286	90

VANILLA, MILK CHOCOLATE, AND HAZELNUT
MARSHMALLOW POPS

MAKES ABOUT 30 MARSHMALLOW LOLLIPOPS

PREPARATION TIME 40 MINUTES
RESTING TIME OVERNIGHT

FOR THE LOLLIPOPS
1 recipe plain marshmallow
(see variation, page 108)
½ vanilla bean, split lengthwise

FOR THE COATING
10½ oz good-quality milk chocolate, chopped
1 cup chopped toasted hazelnuts

MAKING THE MARSHMALLOW
Line an 8-by-8-inch baking dish with parchment paper. As you make the plain marshmallow, scrape the seeds from the vanilla bean into the egg-white mixture along with the gelatin. Pour the mixture into the prepared baking dish, forming a layer about 1¼ inch thick. Cover and allow the marshmallow to set overnight. The next day, cut the marshmallow into 2-by-1-inch cubes and insert a lollipop stick into each one.

COATING THE LOLLIPOPS
Temper the milk chocolate (see page 46). Working one at a time, dip the marshmallows in the chocolate to coat on all sides and tap lightly to remove the excess. Roll in the hazelnuts, then place on an acetate sheet. Allow the chocolate to set for at least 2 hours at 65°F. Detach from the acetate and enjoy. (Store in an airtight container for up to 1 month.)

DARK CHOCOLATE AND STRAWBERRY
MARSHMALLOW POPS

MAKES ABOUT 30 MARSHMALLOW LOLLIPOPS

PREPARATION TIME 40 MINUTES
RESTING TIME OVERNIGHT

FOR THE LOLLIPOPS
1 recipe strawberry marshmallow (see variation, page 108)

FOR THE COATING
2 cups dried strawberries
10½ oz dark chocolate (70% cocoa)

MAKING THE MARSHMALLOW

Line an 8-by-8-inch baking dish with parchment paper. Make the strawberry marshmallow and pour it into the prepared baking dish, making a layer about 1¼ inch thick. Cover and allow the marshmallow to set overnight. The next day, cut the marshmallow into 2-by-1-inch cubes and insert a lollipop stick into each one.

COATING THE LOLLIPOPS

Cut the dried strawberries into small pieces. Temper the dark chocolate (see page 46). Working one at a time, dip the marshmallows in the chocolate to coat on all sides and tap lightly to remove the excess. Top the lollipops with dried strawberry pieces, then place on an acetate sheet. Allow the chocolate to set for at least 2 hours at 65°F. Detach from the acetate and enjoy. (Store the lollipops in an airtight container for up to 1 month.)

DARK CHOCOLATE AND MINT
MARSHMALLOW POPS

MAKES ABOUT 30 MARSHMALLOW LOLLIPOPS

PREPARATION TIME 40 MINUTES
RESTING TIME OVERNIGHT

FOR THE LOLLIPOPS
1 recipe plain marshmallow
(see variation, page 108)
3 drops mint extract
1 pinch of powdered green food coloring (optional)

FOR THE COATING
10½ oz dark chocolate (70% cocoa), chopped
30 crystallized mint leaves (page 134)

MAKING THE MARSHMALLOW
Line an 8-by-8-inch baking dish with parchment paper. Make the plain marshmallow, adding the mint extract and green food coloring after the mixture thickens and cools. Pour the mixture into the prepared baking dish, making a layer about 1¼ inch thick. Cover and allow the marshmallow to set overnight. The next day, cut the marshmallow into 2-by-1-inch cubes and insert a lollipop stick into each one.

COATING THE LOLLIPOPS
Temper the dark chocolate (see page 46). Working one at a time, dip the marshmallows in the chocolate to coat on all sides and tap lightly to remove the excess. Decorate each lollipop with a crystallized mint leaf and place on an acetate sheet. Allow the chocolate to set for at least 2 hours at 65°F. Detach from the acetate and enjoy. (Store the lollipops in an airtight container for up to 1 month.)

LOLLIPOPS

MAKES 20 LOLLIPOPS

PREPARATION TIME 15 MINUTES

1¼ cups sugar
3½ tbsp water
2½ tbsp light corn syrup
Natural flavoring (see the packaging for suggested amounts)
Liquid food coloring for sugar (optional)

PREPARING THE SUGAR SYRUP
In a medium saucepan, combine the sugar and water and bring to a boil over high heat. Add the corn syrup and continue to cook until the mixture registers 250°F on a candy thermometer. Add the natural flavoring and the food coloring (about 10 drops or until mixture reaches the desired hue). Continue to cook over high heat until the syrup registers 310°F. Immediately dip the base of the saucepan in cold water to halt the cooking process.

MAKING THE LOLLIPOPS
Fill twenty 2-inch silicone lollipop molds with the hot sugar syrup. Insert the sticks into the candy. Allow to harden and cool before removing from the molds, and enjoy! (Store the lollipops in an airtight container away from moisture for up to 3 months.)

 CHEF'S TIP: *It's up to you to discover your favorite flavor: orange flower water, rosewater, coffee, vanilla, violet . . .*

BARLEY SUGAR STRAWS

MAKES ABOUT 20 STRAWS

PREPARATION TIME 30 MINUTES

1⅓ cups sugar
3½ tbsp water
2½ tbsp light corn syrup
Natural flavorings (see the packaging for suggested amounts)
Liquid food coloring for sugar (optional)

PREPARING THE SUGAR SYRUP

In a medium saucepan, combine the sugar and water and bring to a boil over high heat. Add the corn syrup and continue to cook until the mixture registers 250°F on a candy thermometer. Add the natural flavoring and continue to cook over high heat until the syrup registers 325°F. Immediately dip the base of the saucepan in cold water to halt the cooking process.

SHAPING THE STRAWS

Working quickly, pour the hot sugar syrup into two pools on a silicone mat. Add a few drops of your choice of food coloring to one of the pools. As the sugar cools, gather up each portion onto itself to make two balls. Be careful, as the sugar will be very hot—we suggest you wear thick rubber gloves. Working with one at a time, pull the balls of sugar by stretching and folding them several times. The sugar will become opaque. Roll each piece into a sausage, twist them together, then roll the twist to form a cylinder about ¼ inch in diameter. Cut into 6-inch lengths and allow to cool completely. (Store in an airtight container away from moisture for up to 2 months.)

 CHEF'S TIP: *If the sugar cools and becomes too hard to roll, you can reheat it briefly in a 250°F oven to make it more malleable.*

CUSTOMER PORTRAITS:
SOPHIE TOPORKOFF

OCCUPATION . . . . Art director
NEIGHBORHOOD . . . . 9th arrondissement
STORE VISITED . . . . Rue du Faubourg-Montmartre
FIRST VISIT . . . . Last year

FREQUENCY OF VISITS . . . . Once a month
FAVORITE CHOCOLATE . . . . Milk and white
CHOCOLATE CONSUMPTION . . . It depends on the day!

1
WHEN DO YOU VISIT THE STORE?
Summer, in the morning. Or winter, at the end of the day.

2
WHAT IS YOUR GREATEST INDULGENCE?
Marrons glacés.

3
WHAT WAS YOUR CHILDHOOD TREAT?
Berlingots.

4
WHAT KIND OF TREATS DO YOU LIKE TO SHARE?
Calissons.

5
THE TREAT YOU ENJOY ALONE?
Caramels!

6
WHAT DO YOU THINK IS THE MOST ROMANTIC TREAT?
The violet-flavored boiled sweets.

7
THE MOST AMUSING TREAT?
The marzipans shaped like tiny piggies.

8
DESCRIBE A PERFECT MOMENT TIED TO A TREAT FROM À LA MÈRE DE FAMILLE.
Last week, my two best friends came to my house and we spent the evening eating *exquimaux* from À la Mère de Famille, swapping them round to try all the flavors.

9
IF LA MÈRE WERE TO GIVE YOU A PRESENT, WHAT WOULD YOU LIKE IT TO BE?
A night all alone with her.

10
WHAT DOES À LA MÈRE DE FAMILLE REPRESENT FOR YOU?
A bottomless well of sweets waiting to be discovered.

11
WHAT DO YOU THINK SHOULD BE THE MOTTO FOR À LA MÈRE DE FAMILLE?
"Big momma thang," like the title of the Lil' Kim song.

12
WHAT IS THE SECRET TO ITS ENDURING SUCCESS?
The recipe for the marrons glacés!

13
WHAT MAKES THE SHOP DIFFERENT FROM OTHERS LIKE IT?
Its window displays—they're the most mouthwatering in Paris.

14
DESCRIBE YOUR FIRST ENCOUNTER.
When I was a child, my best friend lived just next door, so we spent *all* of our time in front of it and scrutinized every square inch of the display window.

15
HAVE YOU EVER BEEN INSPIRED BY A SWEET?
No, but it has often been the reward for an inspiration.

BERLINGOTS

PREPARATION TIME 30 MINUTES
COOKING TIME 15 MINUTES

1⅓ cups sugar
3½ tbsp water
2½ tbsp light corn syrup
Natural flavoring (see the packaging for suggested amounts)
Liquid food coloring for sugar (optional)

PREPARING THE SUGAR SYRUP

In a medium saucepan, combine the sugar and water and bring to a boil over high heat. Add the corn syrup and continue to cook until the mixture registers 250°F on a candy thermometer. Add the natural flavoring and continue to cook over high heat until the syrup registers 325°F. Immediately dip the base of the saucepan in cold water to halt the cooking process.

FORMING THE BERLINGOTS

Working quickly, pour the hot sugar syrup into two pools on a silicone mat. Add a few drops of your choice of food coloring to one of the pools. As the sugar cools, gather up each portion onto itself to make two balls. Be careful, as the mixture will be very hot—we suggest you wear thick rubber gloves. Pull the uncolored ball of sugar by stretching and folding it several times—the sugar will become opaque. Roll this portion into a thin cylinder and arrange it in a zigzag over the colored sugar. Roll the sugar together to make a cylinder that is striped with white sugar. Keep rolling until the cylinder measures ¼ inch in diameter. With a pair of scissors, cut the cylinder at ½-inch intervals, giving the cylinder a quarter turn before each cut, to form the unique berlingot shape. Allow to cool completely, making sure the candies are not touching each other. Store in an airtight container away from moisture for up to 2 months.

CHEF'S TIP: *If the sugar cools and becomes too hard to roll, you can reheat it briefly in a 250°F oven to make it more malleable.*

MINT, VIOLET, OR POPPY
BOILED SWEETS

MAKES ABOUT 50 PIECES

PREPARATION TIME 20 MINUTES
COOKING TIME 15 MINUTES

1⅓ cups granulated sugar
3½ tbsp water
2½ tbsp light corn syrup
3 drops natural mint flavoring,
or 10 drops violet flavoring,
or 10 drops poppy flavoring
Liquid food coloring for sugar (optional)
Confectioners' sugar, for coating

PREPARING THE SUGAR SYRUP

In a medium saucepan, combine the sugar and water and bring to a boil over high heat. Add the corn syrup and continue to cook until the mixture registers 250°F on a candy thermometer. Add the natural flavoring and the food coloring (about 10 drops or until the syrup reaches the desired hue). Continue to cook over high heat until the syrup regisers 310°F. Immediately dip the base of the saucepan in cold water to halt the cooking process.

FORMING THE CANDIES

Working quickly, pour the hot sugar syrup onto a silicone mat. Gather it up onto itself into a ball, then roll it into a cylinder with a ½-inch diameter. Be careful, as the mixture will be very hot—we suggest you wear thick rubber gloves. With a pair of scissors, cut the cylinder at ½-inch intervals. Allow to cool completely, then toss the sweets in confectioners' sugar. Store in an airtight container away from moisture for up to 2 months.

HONEY SWEETS

MAKES ABOUT 30 PIECES

PREPARATION TIME 20 MINUTES
COOKING TIME 15 MINUTES

¾ cup superfine sugar
¼ cup honey
Confectioners' sugar, for coating

PREPARING THE SUGAR SYRUP

In a medium saucepan, combine the superfine sugar and honey and bring to a boil over high heat. Cook until the syrup registers 320°F on a candy thermometer, then immediately dip the base of the saucepan in cold water to halt the cooking process.

FORMING THE CANDIES

Working quickly, pour the hot sugar syrup onto a silicone mat. Gather it up onto itself in a ball, then roll it into a cylinder with a ½-inch diameter. Be careful, as the mixture will be very hot—we suggest you wear thick rubber gloves. With a pair of scissors, cut the cylinder at ½-inch intervals. Allow to cool completely, then toss the sweets in confectioners' sugar. Store in an airtight container away from moisture for up to 2 months.

CHEF'S TIP: *For this recipe, as for most others in this chapter, you will need a candy thermometer, which will help a great deal when cooking the sugar syrup.*

ALMOND-PISTACHIO
NOUGATINE

MAKES A 12 x 12 IN SQUARE

PREPARATION TIME 20 MINUTES

¾ cup sugar
⅓ cup light corn syrup
¾ cup plus 2 tbsp sliced almonds
⅓ cup chopped pistachios
2 tbsp unsalted butter

MAKING THE CARAMEL
Put the sugar and corn syrup in a medium saucepan and follow the cooking instructions on page 8 to make light caramel. When the mixture is pale brown, add the almonds, pistachios, and butter. Mix well to coat the nuts in the caramel and toast them lightly.

MAKING THE NOUGATINE
Working quickly, turn the mixture out onto a sheet of parchment paper or onto a silicone mat. Place a second sheet or mat on top, then roll out the nougatine very thinly with a rolling pin. To finish, cut out the desired shapes using a knife or a pair of scissors. If the nougatine hardens too much to cut, reheat it in a 275°F oven for 4 to 5 minutes to soften it a little. (Store in an airtight container, away from moisture, for up to 1 month.)

VARIATION: *Dipping the nougatine into some chocolate will make this confection even more indulgent. Or process it into crumbs and sprinkle over a summer fruit compote or ice cream.*

CARAMELS

MAKES ABOUT 60 CARAMELS

PREPARATION TIME 35 MINUTES
RESTING TIME OVERNIGHT

SALTED-BUTTER CARAMELS

1⅓ cups whipping cream
1¾ cups plus 2 tbsp sugar
⅔ cup plus 1 tbsp light corn syrup
5 tbsp salted butter

MAKING THE CARAMEL

Warm the cream in a small saucepan over medium heat until it registers about 175°F on an instant-read thermometer. In a medium saucepan, combine the sugar and corn syrup and follow the cooking instructions on page 8 to make a light caramel. Stir in the warm cream until combined. Cook over medium heat, stirring often, until the caramel registers 245°F, then add the butter and stir to combine.

FORMING THE CANDIES

Pour the hot caramel into a small baking sheet lined with parchment paper. Cover and allow to set overnight at room temperature. Cut into 1-inch squares and wrap each one in cellophane like a bonbon. (Store the caramels in an airtight container away from moisture for up to 1 month.)

HAZELNUT CARAMELS

1⅓ cups whipping cream
1¾ cups sugar
¾ cup light corn syrup
4 tbsp praline paste (page 48), made with hazelnuts
3½ tbsp unsalted butter
½ cup chopped skinned, toasted hazelnuts

MAKING THE CARAMEL

Warm the cream in a small saucepan over medium heat until it registers about 175°F on an instant-read thermometer. In a medium saucepan, combine the sugar and corn syrup and follow the cooking instructions on page 8 to make a light caramel. Stir the warm cream until combined, then add the praline paste. Cook over medium heat, stirring often, until the caramel registers 240°F, then add the butter and hazelnuts and stir to combine.

FORMING THE CANDIES

Pour the hot caramel into a small baking sheet lined with parchment paper. Cover and allow to set overnight at room temperature. Cut into 1-inch squares and wrap each one in cellophane like a bonbon. (Store the caramels in an airtight container away from moisture for up to 1 month.)

CHOCOLATE CARAMELS

1⅓ cups whipping cream
¼ cup water
1½ cups sugar
⅓ cup light corn syrup
5½ oz dark chocolate (70% cocoa), chopped
5 tbsp unsalted butter

MAKING THE CARAMEL

Warm the cream in a small saucepan over medium heat until it registers about 175°F on an instant-read thermometer. In a medium saucepan, combine the water, sugar, and corn syrup and follow the cooking instructions on page 8 to make a light caramel. Stir in the warm cream until combined. Cook over medium heat, stirring often, until the caramel registers 235°F, then remove from the heat and add the chocolate and butter and stir to combine.

FORMING THE CANDIES

Pour the hot caramel into a small baking sheet lined with parchment paper. Cover and allow to set overnight at room temperature. Cut into 1-inch squares and wrap each one in cellophane like a bonbon. (Store the caramels in an airtight container away from moisture for up to 1 month.)

CONTINUED

CARAMELS

MAKES ABOUT 60 CARAMELS

**PREPARATION TIME 35 MINUTES
RESTING TIME OVERNIGHT**

PISTACHIO CARAMELS

1⅓ cups whipping cream
1¾ cups sugar
¾ cup light corn syrup
3 tbsp pistachio paste (page 160)
3½ tbsp unsalted butter
¼ cup pistachios

MAKING THE CARAMEL

Warm the cream in a small saucepan over medium heat until it registers about 175°F on an instant-read thermometer. In a medium saucepan, combine the sugar and corn syrup and follow the cooking instructions on page 8 to make a light caramel. Stir in the warm cream until combined, then stir in the pistachio paste. Cook over medium heat, stirring often, until the caramel registers 245°F, then add the butter and pistachios and stir to combine.

FORMING THE CANDIES

Pour the hot caramel into a small baking sheet lined with parchment paper. Cover and allow to set overnight at room temperature. Cut into 1-inch squares and wrap each one in cellophane like a bonbon. (Store the caramels in an airtight container away from moisture for up to 1 month.)

CHERRY CARAMELS

1¾ cups whipping cream
1¼ cups sugar
1 cup light corn syrup
6 oz morello cherries, drained and chopped
2½ tbsp unsalted butter

MAKING THE CARAMEL

Warm the cream in a small saucepan over medium heat until it registers about 175°F on an instant-read thermometer. In a medium saucepan, combine the sugar and corn syrup and follow the cooking instructions on page 8 to make a light caramel. Stir in the warm cream until combined, then stir in the cherries. Cook over medium heat, stirring often, until the caramel registers 245°F, then add the butter and stir to combine.

FORMING THE CANDIES

Pour the hot caramel into a small baking sheet lined with parchment paper. Cover and allow to set overnight at room temperature. Cut into 1-inch squares and wrap each one in cellophane like a bonbon. (Store the caramels in an airtight container away from moisture for up to 1 month.)

PASSION FRUIT CARAMELS

1 cup whipping cream
1½ cups sugar
¾ cup light corn syrup
7 tbsp passion fruit purée
3 tbsp unsalted butter

MAKING THE CARAMEL

Warm the cream in a small saucepan over medium heat until it registers about 175°F on an instant-read thermometer. In a medium saucepan, combine the sugar and corn syrup and follow the cooking instructions on page 8 to make a light caramel. Stir in the warm cream until combined, then stir in the passion fruit purée. Cook until the caramel registers 245°F, then add the butter and stir to combine.

FORMING THE CANDIES

Pour the hot caramel into a small baking sheet lined with parchment paper. Cover and allow to set overnight at room temperature. Cut into 1-inch squares and wrap each one in cellophane like a bonbon. (Store the caramels in an airtight container away from moisture for up to 1 month.)

1850 ~ 1895

1761 ~ 1791
A SHOP WITH THE ALLURE OF A FARMHOUSE

1791 ~ 1807
THE FATE OF LE PÈRE DE FAMILLE

1807 ~ 1825
A FREE WOMAN

1825 ~ 1850
AT THE HEART OF ARTISTIC LIFE

1850 ~ 1895
A NEW ERA OF COOKIES

*

A NEW ERA
OF
COOKIES

In 1856, the Bridauld daughters inherit the shop.

They both come from the world of confectionery, but stay faithful to their father's wishes by deciding to entrust À la Mère de Famille to men versed in the craft of confectionery. Messieurs Noble, Sellier, and Michel, all confectioners by trade, succeed each other at the head of the company until the end of the century, each bringing his know-how and passion. They continue the evolution started by the Bridauld family by contributing new delicacies and sweet specialities and definitively transform the *ancien régime* grocery store into a modern confectionery store. By 1880, À la Mère de Famille is a neighborhood institution, and the shop sells more than 150,000 grocery and confectionery items, the latter being its speciality from this time forward. Flushed with success and now recognized as an establishment for surprising sweets, À la Mère de Famille diversifies futher and very quickly becomes famous for its cookies. At the end of the nineteenth century, the shop becomes one of the very first distributors of the Lefèvre Utile *petit-beurre* cookie, better known as LU. The iconic cookie is featured on the facade of the Rue du Faubourg-Montmartre store (and continues to be to this day).

In the 1860s, the 9th arrondissement puts on a new face with the construction of the Drouot auction house and numerous art stores. The neighborhood regulars at that time go by the names of Émile Zola, Gustave Flaubert, Paul Cézanne, and Edmond and Jules de Goncourt. The Folies Trévise, an opera house, is established in 1869, just a few steps away from the store. This building receives its definitive name in 1872: the Folies-Bergère. The dancers from this cabaret become regular customers and baskets of sweets are delivered to them in their dressing rooms nightly.

ROUDOUDOUS

~~~~~~~~~~~~~~~~

MAKES ABOUT 40 PIECES
PREPARATION TIME 20 MINUTES

~~~~~~~~~~~~~~~~

sugar .... 1¼ cups
water .... 3½ tbsp
light corn syrup .... 2½ tbsp
natural flavoring (see the packaging for suggested amounts)
liquid food coloring for sugar

PREPARING THE SHELLS

Preheat the oven to 350°F. Scrub about 40 small clam and/or cockle half-shells. Set them on a baking sheet and dry them in the oven for 10 minutes.

COOKING

In a medium saucepan, combine the sugar and water and bring to a boil over high heat. Add the corn syrup and continue to cook until the mixture registers 250°F on a candy thermometer. Add the natural flavoring and the food coloring (about 10 drops or until the syrup reaches the desired hue). Continue to cook over high heat until the syrup registers 310°F. Immediately dip the base of the saucepan in cold water to halt the cooking process. Working quickly, pour the hot sugar syrup into the shells. Allow to harden and cool before serving. (Store in an airtight container for up to 1 week.)

CHOCOLATE-CARAMEL LOLLIPOPS

MAKES ABOUT 20 LOLLIPOPS

PREPARATION TIME 40 MINUTES

FOR THE LOLLIPOPS
¾ cup plus 2 tbsp whipping cream
¾ cup sugar
½ cup light corn syrup
3½ tbsp unsalted butter

FOR DIPPING
10½ oz dark (70% cocoa), milk,
or white chocolate, chopped

MAKING THE CARAMEL
In a small saucepan over medium heat, warm the cream until it registers about 175°F on an instant-read thermometer. In a medium saucepan, combine the sugar and corn syrup and follow the cooking instructions on page 8 to make a light caramel. Stir in the warm cream until combined. Cook over medium heat, stirring often, until the caramel registers 250°F, then add the butter and stir to combine.

MAKING THE LOLLIPOPS
Pour the hot caramel into a baking sheet lined with a silicone mat. Allow to cool, then cut into 1-by-3-inch rectangles. Insert a lollipop stick into each caramel rectangle. Temper the chocolate (see page 46). Dip each lollipop into the chocolate to coat, allow excess to drip off, then place on an acetate sheet. Allow to set, then detach from the sheet and enjoy. (Store in an airtight container for up to 1 week.)

MONTÉLIMAR NOUGAT

MAKES 6 SLICES

PREPARATION TIME 30 MINUTES
RESTING TIME OVERNIGHT

½ cup plus 2 tbsp honey
1⅓ cups plus 1 tbsp sugar
1 tbsp light corn syrup
3 tbsp water
1 egg white
1½ cups unblanched almonds, toasted
¼ cup pistachios

MAKING THE NOUGAT

Line a 9-by-4-inch loaf pan with parchment paper. In a medium saucepan, warm the honey over medium-high heat until it registers 255°F on a candy thermometer. In a separate medium saucepan, combine the 1⅓ cups sugar, corn syrup, and water and cook over medium-high heat until the mixture registers 285°F, swirling occasionally. Meanwhile, in the clean, dry bowl of a stand mixer, whip the egg white and remaining 1 tbsp sugar on low speed with the whisk attachment until foamy. With the mixer running, slowly pour in the warm honey, followed by the hot sugar syrup. Continue beating on low speed for 5 minutes more, until the mixture is lukewarm. Meanwhile, heat the almonds and pistachios in a medium frying pan over medium heat, stirring occasionally, until warm to the touch. To check if the nougat is ready, scoop up a small amount with a spoon and dip it into cold water; it should form a firm ball. Add the warm nuts to the nougat and fold with a spatula until well combined.

FINISHING

Spoon the nougat into the prepared loaf pan, cover, and allow to cool overnight at room temperature. The next day, remove the nougat from the pan and, with a serrated knife, cut it lengthwise into 6 slices. Wrap each slice in plastic wrap to protect it from humidity. (Store in an airtight container for up to 1 week.)

 CHEF'S TIP: *The darker the honey, the more pronounced its flavor will be in the nougat.*

NOUGAT NOIR

MAKES AN 8 x 8 IN SQUARE

PREPARATION TIME 30 MINUTES

2 cups unblanched almonds
1½ cups hazelnuts
¾ cup honey
¾ cup sugar

MAKING THE NOUGAT

Preheat the oven to 325°F. Place the almonds and hazelnuts on a baking sheet and toast for 10 minutes. Remove from the oven and set aside. Combine the honey and sugar in a large saucepan and follow the instructions on page 8 to make a dark caramel. Add the almonds and hazelnuts to the caramel, mixing well to combine.

FINISHING

Pour the caramel into a baking sheet lined with parchment paper and allow to cool completely. Break the nougat into pieces to serve. (Store in an airtight container away from moisture for up to 1 month.)

There is nothing like homemade nougat noir, prettily wrapped, to offer as a gift at Christmastime. This confection has the advantage of being very quick to prepare. It has a hard consistency, like a brittle, and is very delicious—a treat that is hard to resist!

PISTACHIO NOUGAT

MAKES 6 SLICES

PREPARATION TIME 30 MINUTES
RESTING TIME OVERNIGHT

½ cup plus 2 tbsp honey
1⅓ cups plus 1 tbsp sugar
1 tbsp light corn syrup
3 tbsp water
1 egg white
2 tbsp pistachio paste (page 160)
1½ cups unblanched almonds, toasted
1½ cups pistachios

MAKING THE NOUGAT

Line a 9-by-4-inch loaf pan with parchment paper. In a medium saucepan, warm the honey over medium-high heat until it registers 255°F on a candy thermometer. In a separate medium saucepan, combine the 1⅓ cups sugar, corn syrup, and water and cook over medium-high heat until the mixture registers 285°F, swirling occasionally. Meanwhile, in the clean, dry bowl of a stand mixer, whip the egg white and remaining 1 tbsp sugar on low speed with the whisk attachment until foamy. With the mixer running, slowly pour in the warm honey, followed by the hot sugar syrup. Continue beating on low speed for 5 minutes more, until the mixture is lukewarm. Meanwhile, heat the almonds and pistachios in a medium frying pan over medium heat, stirring occasionally, until warm to the touch. Add the pistachio paste to the egg-white mixture and beat until combined. To check if the nougat is ready, scoop up a small amount with a spoon and dip it into cold water; it should form a firm ball. Add the warm nuts to the nougat and fold with a spatula until well combined.

FINISHING

Spoon the nougat into the prepared pan, cover, and allow to cool overnight at room temperature. The next day, remove the nougat from the pan and, with a serrated knife, cut it lengthwise into 6 slices. Wrap each slice in plastic wrap to protect it from humidity. Store in an airtight container for up to 1 week.

CHEF'S TIP: *Pistachio paste can sometimes be found in specialty grocery stores. You can also make it yourself (see page 160).*

4

THIS CHAPTER CONTAINS recipes for making many different types of candied fruit, as well as *pâtes de fruits*, or fruit jellies. You can enjoy these sweet treats all by themselves or use them in cakes or chocolate creations. Good candied fruit is sometimes difficult to find and can be expensive. Making it yourself guarantees flavor and freshness that will make all the difference in your baking. In this chapter, you will also find recipes for marzipan and pistachio paste, both of which offer endless possibilities in the sweet kitchen.

CANDIED FRUITS
AND SUCH

MARZIPAN

MAKES ABOUT 1 POUND

PREPARATION TIME 15 MINUTES

1¾ cups ground almonds or almond meal
1 cup sugar
¼ cup light corn syrup
⅓ cup water

MAKING THE PASTE

Put the ground almonds in a food processor. In a medium saucepan, combine the sugar, corn syrup, and water and cook over medium-high heat until the syrup registers 250°F on a candy thermometer. With the food processor running, slowly pour the hot sugar syrup through the feed tube and continue to process until the mixture forms a smooth paste.

FINISHING

Transfer the paste to a clean bowl and set aside until cool enough to handle. Using your hands, work the paste into a log shape. Store the marzipan in the refrigerator for up to 1 month.

 USES: *Marzipan can be used as a filling for chocolates or to stuff dried fruits. But first, combine the marzipan with a little liqueur, pistachio paste (page 160), or coffee extract to vary the flavor.*

PISTACHIO PASTE

MAKES ABOUT 1 POUND

PREPARATION TIME 15 MINUTES

1½ cups blanched pistachios
½ cup sugar
2 tbsp water
1½ tbsp orgeat syrup (see chef's tip)
2 tbsp plus 1 tsp hazelnut oil

PREPARING THE SUGAR SYRUP

Preheat the oven to 325°F. Place the pistachios on a baking sheet and roast for 10 minutes. Remove from the oven and set aside. In a medium saucepan, combine the sugar and water and cook over medium-high heat until the syrup registers 250°F on a candy thermometer.

MAKING THE PASTE

Put the pistachios in a food processor and process until they are finely ground. With the food processor running, slowly pour the hot sugar syrup through the feed tube and continue to process until combined. Add the orgeat syrup and hazelnut oil and continue to process until the mixture forms a smooth paste. Transfer to an airtight container. Store the pistachio paste in the refrigerator for up to 1 month.

 CHEF'S TIP: *Orgeat syrup is an almond-flavored syrup that is often used in cocktails. It is available in most good liquor stores. You can use this pistachio paste in many ways—try making a pistachio-based cream instead of an almond-based frangipane in a pear tart. Mmm . . .*

CALISSONS

MAKES ABOUT 30 PIECES

PREPARATION TIME 30 MINUTES
RESTING TIME OVERNIGHT

FOR THE CALISSON PASTE
⅔ cup candied melon
¼ cup candied orange peel (page 102)
4 or 5 drops orange flower water
2 cups ground almonds or almond meal
1½ tbsp honey
½ cup superfine sugar
3 tbsp water

1 sheet of wafer paper

FOR THE ICING
1 egg white
1 cup confectioners' sugar

MAKING THE CALISSON PASTE

Add the candied fruits and orange flower water to a food processor and process to combine, then add the ground almonds and honey and pulse to incorporate. In a medium saucepan, combine the superfine sugar and water and cook over medium-high heat until the syrup registers 250°F on a candy thermometer. Pour the hot sugar syrup into the food processor and process for about 2 minutes, until the mixture forms a smooth paste.

ASSEMBLY

Turn the paste out onto the sheet of wafer paper. Cover with a sheet of parchment paper, then roll out the paste with a rolling pin to a thickness of ½ inch. Remove the parchment and allow the paste to dry overnight at room temperature.

MAKING THE ICING

In a medium bowl, whisk together the egg white and confectioners' sugar. (The icing must be smooth and spreadable, and neither too hard nor too soft. If too thin, add more confectioners' sugar; if too thick, add more egg white to achieve the correct consistency.) With a pastry cutter or knife, cut the desired shapes. Spread the shapes with icing using a small offset spatula, set them on a baking sheet, and place in the oven for 5 minutes to dry. Remove from the oven and allow to cool completely. (Store in an airtight container for up to 1 month.)

 VARIATION: *To vary the flavor, you can add other candied fruits or replace some of the candied orange with dried fruit such as dates, apricots, and figs.*

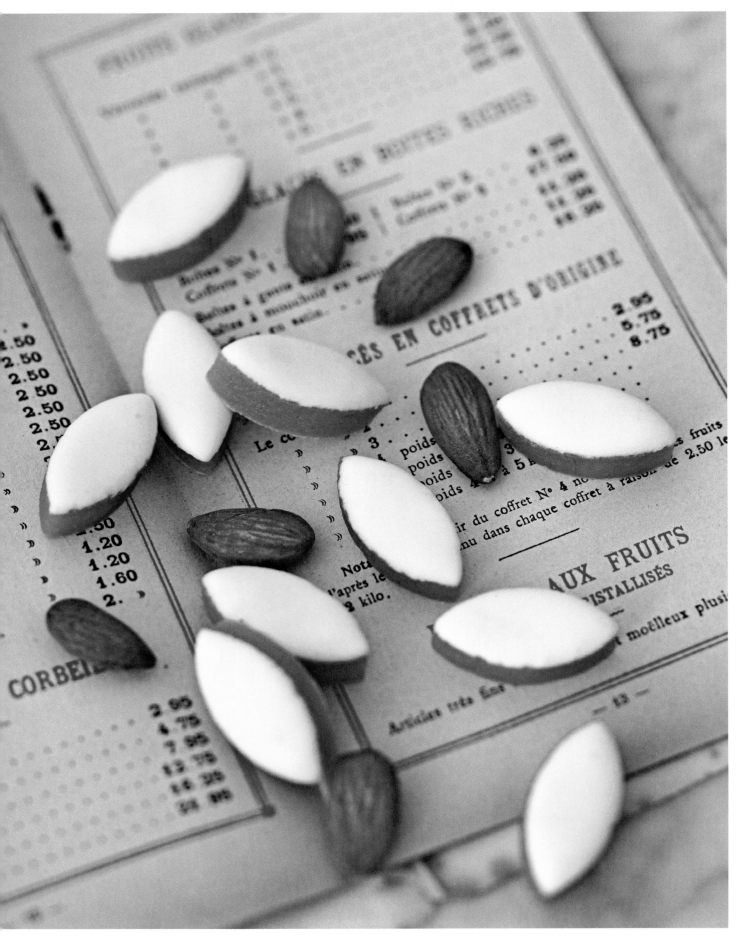

1895
~
1920

1761 ~ 1791

A SHOP WITH THE ALLURE OF A FARMHOUSE

1791 ~ 1807

THE FATE OF LE PÈRE DE FAMILLE

1807 ~ 1825

A FREE WOMAN

1825 ~ 1850

AT THE HEART OF ARTISTIC LIFE

1850 ~ 1895

A NEW ERA OF COOKIES

A CHILDHOOD DREAM COME TRUE

~~~~~~~~~~

E ver since he was a young boy, Georges Lecœur was a frequent visitor to the Faubourg-Montmartre quarter and its famous confectionery store.

Fascinated by the shop, he makes a boyhood promise to himself that he will own it one day. He goes on to study biology, then moves into the neighborhood and buys a shop on Rue Cadet so he can work in proximity to the confectionery store he covets. When that store is put up for sale a few years later, Georges Lecœur wastes no time in buying it, fulfilling his childhood dream. À la Mère de Famille is finally his. His scientific knowledge greatly influences the changes he makes. He renovates the facade, installs a telephone, produces the shop's first advertisements and brochures, pushes for gastronomic innovations, and, for the first time, offers products from all over the world: *hopjes* from Holland, chocolate imported from the tropics, teas from China, raisins from Andalusia.

À la Mère de Famille becomes a shop of rare and surprising pleasures, combining creativity, authenticity, and indulgence, and uniting fine food lovers of all generations. It is this period of discovery and development that inspires the store that exists today. In 1907, Georges Lecœur approaches a young man he has seen working in the neighborhood. Thus Régis Dreux begins his career with À la Mère de Famille—and he absorbs all of Georges' passion. Over the years, the two men become close friends. But when World War I breaks out, Régis Dreux has to leave for the front. Before he departs, Georges, who has not been able to persuade his son to take over the shop, promises it to his young apprentice. Régis Dreux survives the war and returns to Paris. When his employer and friend dies, he takes the reins of the establishment.

~~~~~~~~~~

The Belle Époque has Paris in a state of exuberance. The World Fairs of 1889 and 1900 leave the capital with two enduring landmarks: the Eiffel Tower and the Grand Palais. Professionals of the food trade now have a salon: the Exposition Internationale Culinaire d'Alimentation et d'Hygiène de Paris. Georges Lecœur is singled out on two occasions, in 1900 and in 1906, for the excellence of his preserves.

LEMON MIDINETTES

MAKES ABOUT **20** COOKIES
PREPARATION TIME **35** MINUTES
BAKING TIME **10** MINUTES

COOKIES

eggs, separated	3
granulated sugar	½ cup
all-purpose flour	½ cup
confectioners' sugar	for dusting

ICING AND FILLING

water	3½ tbsp
granulated sugar	½ cup
lemon juice	1½ tbsp
confectioners' sugar	1½ cups
yellow food coloring	5 drops
lemon marmalade	1⅓ cups

MAKING THE COOKIES

Line a baking sheet with parchment paper and fit a piping bag with a ½-inch plain tip. In the dry bowl of a stand mixer, whip the egg whites to soft peaks. With the mixer running, gradually add the granulated sugar and continue to beat until stiff peaks form. Using a spatula, fold in the egg yolks. Sift the flour over and fold to combine.

BAKING

Preheat the oven to 350°F. Fill the piping bag with batter and pipe 2-inch mounds onto the prepared baking sheet. Sift confectioners' sugar over the top and bake for 6 to 8 minutes, or until the cookies are a lovely golden color. Remove from the oven, cool on a wire rack, then use a 1½-inch round pastry cutter to cut each cookie into a neat circle. Turn down the oven temperature to 325°F.

ICING AND FILLING

Combine the water and granulated sugar in a medium saucepan over medium heat, stirring until the sugar dissolves. Stir in the lemon juice, confectioners' sugar, and a few drops of food coloring. Sandwich 1 tbsp of lemon marmalade between two cookies. Repeat. Place the cookies on a rack and spoon the icing over the top. Store in an airtight container for up to 3 days.

STRAWBERRY PÂTE DE FRUITS

MAKES ABOUT 50 PIECES

PREPARATION TIME 30 MINUTES
RESTING TIME OVERNIGHT

1²⁄₃ cups strawberry purée
3½ tsp yellow pectin
¼ cup plus 6 tbsp sugar, plus more for coating
⅓ cup honey
⅓ cup lemon juice

MAKING THE PÂTE DE FRUITS

Line a rimmed baking sheet with parchment paper. In a medium saucepan, warm the strawberry purée over medium-low heat until it registers 120°F on an instant-read thermometer. In a separate medium saucepan, combine the pectin and ¼ cup sugar. Add the warm strawberry purée, bring to a boil over high heat, and boil for 1 minute. Add the remaining 6 tbsp sugar, bring back to a boil, then stir in the honey and continue cooking until the mixture registers 225°F. Stir in the lemon juice to halt the cooking process. Immediately pour the mixture into the prepared baking sheet and let set overnight at room temperature.

CUTTING UP AND COATING

Turn the solid slab out onto a cutting board and peel off the parchment. Sprinkle a little sugar on both sides of the square. Cut into 1-inch squares and finish by rolling the squares in sugar. Store in an airtight container at room temperature for up to 1 month.

VARIATION: *To change things up, replace the strawberry purée with an equal amount of raspberry purée.*

MANGO-PASSION FRUIT PÂTE DE FRUITS

MAKES ABOUT 50 PIECES

PREPARATION TIME 30 MINUTES
RESTING TIME OVERNIGHT

1 cup plus 1 tbsp mango purée
⅔ cup strained passion fruit purée
4 tsp yellow pectin
¼ cup plus 6 tbsp sugar, plus more for coating
⅓ cup honey
⅓ cup lemon juice

MAKING THE PÂTE DE FRUITS

Line a rimmed baking sheet with parchment paper. In a medium saucepan, combine the mango and passion fruit purée and heat over medium-low heat until the mixture registers 120°F on an instant-read thermometer. In a separate medium saucepan, combine the pectin and ¼ cup sugar. Add the warm mango mixture over medium-high heat, bring to a boil, and boil for 1 minute. Add the remaining 6 tbsp sugar, bring back to a boil, then stir in the honey and continue cooking until the mixture registers 225°F. Stir in the lemon juice to halt the cooking process. Immediately pour the mixture into the prepared baking sheet and let set overnight at room temperature.

CUTTING UP AND COATING

Turn the solid slab out onto a cutting board and peel off the parchment. Sprinkle a little sugar on both sides of the square. Cut into 1-inch squares and finish by rolling the squares in sugar. Store in an airtight container at room temperature for up to 1 month.

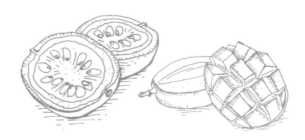

LYCHEE PÂTE DE FRUITS

MAKES ABOUT 50 PIECES

PREPARATION TIME 30 MINUTES
RESTING TIME OVERNIGHT

1²⁄₃ cups lychee purée
4 tsp yellow pectin
¼ cup plus 6 tbsp sugar, plus more for coating
⅓ cup honey
⅓ cup lemon juice

MAKING THE PÂTE DE FRUITS

Line a rimmed baking sheet with parchment paper. In a medium saucepan, warm the lychee purée over medium-low heat until it registers 120°F on an instant-read thermometer. In a separate medium saucepan, combine the pectin and ¼ cup sugar. Add the warm lychee purée, bring to a boil over high heat, and boil for 1 minute. Add the remaining 6 tbsp sugar, bring back to a boil, then stir in the honey and continue cooking until the mixture registers 225°F. Stir in the lemon juice to halt the cooking process. Immediately pour the mixture into the prepared baking sheet and let set overnight at room temperature.

CUTTING UP AND COATING

Turn the solid slab out onto a cutting board and peel off the parchment. Sprinkle a little sugar on both sides of the square. Cut into 1-inch squares and finish by rolling the squares in sugar. Store in an airtight container at room temperature for up to 1 month.

PEAR PÂTE DE FRUITS

MAKES ABOUT 50 PIECES

PREPARATION TIME 30 MINUTES
RESTING TIME OVERNIGHT

1⅔ cups pear purée
3½ tsp yellow pectin
¼ cup plus 6 tbsp sugar, plus more for coating
⅓ cup honey
⅓ cup lemon juice

MAKING THE PÂTE DE FRUITS

Line a rimmed baking sheet with parchment paper. In a medium saucepan, warm the pear purée over medium-low heat until it registers 120°F on an instant-read thermometer. In a separate medium saucepan, combine the pectin and ¼ cup sugar. Add the warm pear purée, bring to a boil over high heat, and boil for 1 minute. Add the remaining sugar, bring back to a boil, then stir in the honey and continue cooking until the mixture registers 225°F. Stir in the lemon juice to halt the cooking process. Immediately pour the mixture into the prepared baking sheet and let set overnight at room temperature.

CUTTING AND COATING

Turn the solid slab out onto a cutting board and peel off the parchment. Sprinkle a little sugar on both sides of the square. Cut into 1-inch squares and finish by rolling the squares in sugar. Store in an airtight container at room temperature for up to 1 month.

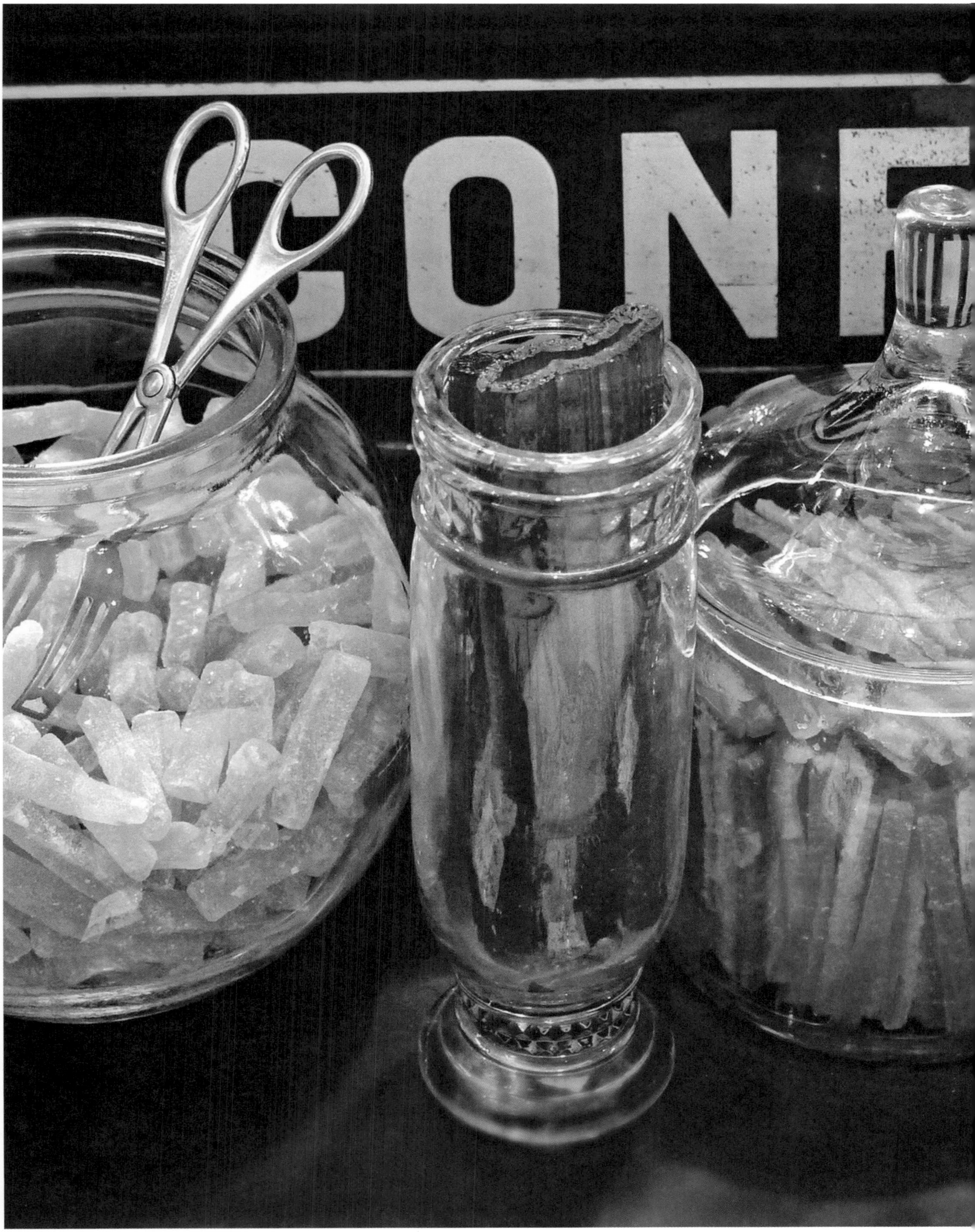
CONF

QUINCE PASTE

MAKES ABOUT 50 PIECES

PREPARATION TIME 2 HOURS
RESTING TIME OVERNIGHT

2¼ lbs quince
3 cups water
Superfine sugar
1 vanilla bean, split lengthwise

PREPARING THE QUINCE

Wash the quince, then peel. Chop the flesh, reserving the seeds. Put the flesh and the water into a medium saucepan. Tie the seeds in a square of cheesecloth and add to the pan. Bring to a simmer over medium heat and cook for 20 minutes, or until the fruit has softened.

MAKING THE QUINCE PASTE

Drain the quince syrup in a colander lined with a layer of cheesecloth; discard the seeds (the juice can be used to make quince jelly). Put the fruit into a food processor and process to a smooth purée. Weigh the purée, then place in a large saucepan. Add the same weight of sugar to a pan. Scrape the seeds from the vanilla bean into the pan, drop in the pods, and cook for 20 minutes over medium-high heat, stirring regularly with a wooden spoon, until thick. Remove from the heat and discard the vanilla pods.

FINISHING

Pour the quince paste into a baking sheet lined with parchment paper to make a ½-inch thick layer. Refrigerate for 24 hours before turning out of the baking sheet and cutting into 1-inch cubes. (Quince paste can be stored in an airtight container at room temperature for up to 3 months.)

USES: *Perhaps the very best of all the* pâtes de fruits, *quince paste is wonderful spread on a piece of toast with some sheep's-milk cheese.*

CANDIED PINEAPPLE

MAKES 1 CANDIED PINEAPPLE

PREPARATION TIME 10 MINUTES OVER 4 DAYS
RESTING TIME 4 NIGHTS + 1 WEEK

1 pineapple
4 cups water
6 cups superfine sugar

PREPARING THE PINEAPPLE

If you are using a small Victoria pineapple, leave the greens attached and remove the skin, but keep the fruit whole. Otherwise, peel the pineapple, taking care to remove all of the eyes, then cut the pineapple crosswise into slices ½ inch thick. Remove the center with a round cutter. Place the whole pineapple in a deep bowl or arrange the slices in a single layer in a large, wide nonreactive dish.

SOAKING IN THE SYRUP

In a medium saucepan, combine the water and 3 cups of the sugar and bring to a boil over high heat. Pour the boiling syrup over the pineapple, cover, and set aside overnight.

COOKING AND STEEPING

The next day, pour the syrup into a large saucepan, add 1 cup sugar, and bring to a boil. Add the pineapple to the syrup, boil for 3 minutes, then remove from the heat, cover, and set aside overnight. Repeat this process two more times over two more days, adding 1 cup sugar to the syrup each time, then allow the pineapple to steep in the syrup for 1 week at room temperature. Remove from the syrup and enjoy!

LEVEL OF DIFFICULTY: *As with all candied fruits, the process for candying pineapple stretches out over a week, but it is very simple and the individual steps don't take much time!*

Dragées
Amandes Extra Fines

3F40

A LA MÈRE DE FAMILLE
Maison fondée en 1761
MAGASIN SPÉCIAL DE DESSERTS D'HIVER

G. LECŒUR
85, Faubourg Montmartre et 1, Rue de Provence
Téléphone : Gutenberg 25-46

A LA MÈRE DE FAMILLE
CONFISERIE & DESSERTS
VINS FINS - LIQUEURS - CHAMPAGNES

—◇—

Ancienne maison R. LEGRAND

A. BRETHONNEAU
35, Faubourg Montmartre et 1, Rue de Provence

PARIS (9e), Mois de Décembre 1963

Maison Fondée en 1761

R. C. SEINE 57 A 16.279
C. C. P. PARIS 10.800 06

Tél. : PROvence 83-69

Jm : 697 75 1093038

Madame Marie Louise Glacier
Extra   Doit

	Salaire brut 20 jours ×		25	500 -
Retenues	Sécurité Sociale 6 %			30
				470 -
	Assurance Chomage 0.05			0 25
				469 75
Indemnité	Transport			16
				485 75

CANDIED KUMQUATS

MAKES ABOUT 30 PIECES

PREPARATION TIME 10 MINUTES OVER 4 DAYS
RESTING TIME 4 NIGHTS + 1 WEEK

1 lb kumquats
4 cups water
6 cups superfine sugar

PREPARING THE KUMQUATS

Wash the kumquats. Bring a large saucepan of water to a boil over high heat, immerse the kumquats, and cook for 5 minutes to soften the skins. Drain well.

SOAKING IN THE SYRUP

In a medium saucepan, combine the 4 cups water and 3 cups of the sugar and bring to a boil over high heat. Place the kumquats in the syrup and cook for 1 minute. Remove from the heat, cover, and set aside overnight.

COOKING AND STEEPING

The next day, pour the syrup into a second medium saucepan, add 1 cup sugar, and bring to a boil over high heat. Immerse the kumquats in the syrup, boil for 3 minutes, then remove from the heat, cover, and set aside overnight. Repeat this process two more times over two more days, adding 1 cup sugar to the syrup each time, then allow the fruit to steep in the syrup for 1 week. Remove from the syrup and enjoy!

CANDIED PEARS

PREPARATION TIME 10 MINUTES OVER 4 DAYS
RESTING TIME 4 NIGHTS + 1 WEEK

3 pears
Juice of 1 lemon
4 cups water
6 cups sugar

PREPARING THE PEARS

Peel the pears and cut them in half, leaving the stems intact. Arrange them in a single layer in a large dish and sprinkle with the lemon juice to prevent them from browning.

SOAKING IN THE SYRUP

In a medium saucepan, combine the water and 3 cups of the sugar and bring to a boil over high heat. Pour the boiling syrup over the pears, cover, and set aside.

COOKING AND STEEPING

The next day, pour the syrup into a large saucepan, add 1 cup sugar, and bring to a boil over high heat. Immerse the pears in the syrup, boil for 3 minutes, then remove from the heat, cover, and set aside overnight. Repeat this process two more times over two more days, adding 1 cup sugar to the syrup each time, then allow the fruit to steep for 1 week. Remove from the syrup and enjoy!

 CHEF'S TIP: *Choose a pear variety that is small in size. For candying, the fruits should not be too green, nor too ripe. It's best to purchase underripe pears and wait for the right moment to use them.*

CANDIED ORANGE AND LEMON SLICES

MAKES ABOUT 40 SLICES

PREPARATION TIME 10 MINUTES OVER 4 DAYS
RESTING TIME 4 NIGHTS + 1 WEEK

4 oranges
4 lemons
4 cups water
6 cups superfine sugar

PREPARING THE ORANGES AND LEMONS

Wash the oranges and lemons and pat dry with paper towels. Cut each fruit crosswise into 1/3-inch slices. Bring a large saucepan of water to a boil over high heat. Immerse the orange and lemon slices and cook for 5 minutes to soften the skins. Drain well, then place in a large, wide nonreactive dish.

SOAKING IN THE SYRUP

In a medium saucepan, combine the 4 cups water and 3 cups of the sugar and bring to a boil over high heat. Pour the boiling syrup over the orange and lemon slices, cover, and set aside.

COOKING AND STEEPING

The next day, pour the syrup into a medium saucepan, add 1 cup sugar, and bring to a boil again over high heat. Immerse the citrus slices in the syrup, boil for 3 minutes, then remove from the heat, cover, and set aside overnight. Repeat this process two more times over two more days, adding 1 cup sugar to the syrup each time, then allow the fruit to steep for 1 week. Remove from the syrup and enjoy!

USES: *These candied orange and lemon slices can be used instead of candied peel in recipes. Since they include both the inside and the outside of the fruit, they are not as bitter as the peel alone.*

CUSTOMER PORTRAITS:
COLETTE LAURY

OCCUPATION . . . . Psychologist
NEIGHBORHOOD . . . . 18ᵗʰ arrondissement
STORE VISITED . . . . Rue du Faubourg-Montmartre
FIRST VISIT . . . . Five years ago

FREQUENCY OF VISITS . . . . Three times a year
FAVORITE CHOCOLATE . . . . Dark
CHOCOLATE CONSUMPTION: . . . . With coffee

1
WHEN DO YOU VISIT THE STORE?
At Christmas or for birthdays.

2
WHAT IS YOUR GREATEST INDULGENCE?
Caramels.

3
YOUR GUILTY PLEASURE?
Marrons glacés.

4
WHAT WAS YOUR CHILDHOOD TREAT?
Carambars.

5
WHAT KIND OF TREATS DO YOU LIKE TO SHARE?
A box of chocolates.

6
DO YOU HAVE A MEMORY CONNECTED TO THIS PLACE?
The pleasure of passing by the window display.

7
DESCRIBE A PERFECT MOMENT TIED TO A TREAT FROM À LA MÈRE DE FAMILLE.
A *pain d'épice* shared between friends during afternoon tea.

8
IF LA MÈRE WERE TO GIVE YOU A PRESENT, WHAT WOULD YOU LIKE IT TO BE?
Palets Montmartre.

9
WHAT DOES À LA MÈRE DE FAMILLE REPRESENT FOR YOU?
The most refined chocolatier in the French tradition.

10
WHAT DO YOU THINK SHOULD BE THE MOTTO OF À LA MÈRE DE FAMILLE?
"Childhood dreams."

11
WHAT IS THE SECRET TO ITS ENDURING SUCCESS?
Attending to the subtlety and finesse of the products while continuing the tradition.

12
WHAT MAKES THE SHOP DIFFERENT FROM THE OTHERS LIKE IT?
The taste of its products is so subtle and refined.

13
DESCRIBE YOUR FIRST ENCOUNTER.
Thrilling.

14
WHAT DOES THE STORE'S HISTORY EVOKE FOR YOU?
Quality in the French tradition.

15
WHY DO YOU LOVE À LA MÈRE DE FAMILLE?
For its incredible sweetness!

MARRONS GLACÉS

MAKES 10 PIECES

PREPARATION TIME 45 MINUTES
CANDYING TIME 10 MINUTES A DAY OVER 7 DAYS

FOR THE CANDIED CHESTNUTS
2¼ lbs fresh chestnuts in their shells
4 cups water
10 cups granulated sugar
1 vanilla bean, split lengthwise

FOR THE ICING
4 cups confectioners' sugar
⅓ cup syrup reserved from candying
the chestnuts

PREPARING THE CHESTNUTS

Rinse the chestnuts. With a sharp paring knife, cut an X into the base of each. Place in a saucepan of water, bring to a boil over high heat, and boil for 3 minutes. Using a slotted spoon, transfer to a plate; keep the water at a boil. When the chestnuts are cool enough to handle, peel off the outer shells. Return the nuts to the boiling water and cook for 15 minutes. Remove from the heat. Working one at a time, remove the chestnuts from the water and, while still hot, peel off the thin inner skin. Drain the peeled chestnuts.

MAKING THE SYRUP

In a large saucepan, combine the water and granulated sugar. Scrape the seeds from the vanilla bean into the pan, add the pods, and bring to a boil over high heat. Add the chestnuts to the syrup, turn down the heat, and simmer gently for 3 minutes. Cover and set aside overnight at room temperature. The next day, remove the chestnuts, bring the syrup to a boil, and boil for 5 minutes to concentrate its sugar content. Immerse the chestnuts in the syrup, turn down the heat, and simmer again for 3 minutes. Cover and set aside overnight. Repeat the process five more times over five more days. The chestnuts are candied when the syrup has soaked through to the center; cut one open to see. Transfer the chestnuts to a wire rack and drain for 12 hours at room temperature; reserve ⅓ cup of the syrup for icing.

ICING THE CHESTNUTS

Preheat the oven to 425°F. In a bowl, whisk together the confectioners' sugar and chestnut syrup. Spoon icing onto each chestnut, allowing the excess to run off. Place in the oven for 2 to 3 minutes to harden the icing. Allow to cool on the rack. (Store in an airtight container away from moisture for up to 1 month.)

5

A SIMPLE SLICE OF BREAD TRANSPORTS US TO HEAVEN WHEN TOPPED WITH ANY ONE OF THE SPREADS IN THIS CHAPTER. With temptations such as classic raspberry jam, milk jam, homemade chocolate spreads that you can customize to suit your taste, caramel spreads, and the lesser-known *sirop de Liège*, there's no chance of getting bored at breakfast time. Fill your shelves with these pots of magic, cooked up in a few simple steps—you will see, they won't last very long.

PÂTE-
S À
TART-
INER

JAMS AND SPREADS

SALTED BUTTER-VANILLA CARAMEL

MAKES 2 CUPS

PREPARATION TIME 20 MINUTES

1½ cups whipping cream
½ vanilla bean, split lengthwise
1½ cups sugar
7 tbsp salted butter

STERILIZING THE JARS

Sterilize a 2-pint canning jar and lid by immersing it in boiling water for 3 minutes. Drain and dry on a rack before using.

INFUSING THE CREAM AND MAKING THE CARAMEL

Put the cream in a medium saucepan and scrape in the seeds from the vanilla bean. (Discard the pod or save for another use.) Heat the mixture over medium heat until it registers about 175°F on an instant-read thermometer. Add the sugar to a large saucepan and follow the instructions on page 8 to make a light caramel. Stop the caramelization of the sugar by adding the hot cream (be careful as it will spatter). Continue to cook the caramel to 225°F, stirring to combine, then stir in the butter. Transfer the mixture to a food processor and process until completely smooth. Spoon the caramel into the prepared jar and seal. Store in the refrigerator for up to 1 week. Bring to room temperature before serving.

HAZELNUT SPREAD

MAKES ABOUT 1 CUP

PREPARATION TIME 30 MINUTES

1½ cups hazelnuts
1¼ cups whole milk
1½ tbsp honey
10 oz good-quality milk chocolate, chopped
2 oz dark chocolate (70% cocoa), chopped

STERILIZING THE JARS

Sterilize a 2-pint canning jar and lid by immersing it in boiling water for 3 minutes. Drain and dry on a rack before using.

PREPARING THE HAZELNUTS

Preheat the oven to 325°F. Place the hazelnuts on a baking sheet and toast for 10 minutes. Remove from the oven, allow to cool, then rub the nuts in a clean dish towel to remove the skins. Process the nuts in a food processor until it forms a smooth paste. Transfer the paste to a large bowl.

MAKING THE SPREAD

In a medium saucepan, combine the milk and honey and bring to a boil over high heat, then pour this mixture over the hazelnut paste. In a double boiler, melt together the milk and dark chocolates, then incorporate them into the hazelnut mixture, stirring to combine. Spoon the hazelnut spread the prepared jar and seal. Store in the refrigerator for up to 1 week. Bring to room temperature before using.

 VARIATION: *This recipe accommodates all sorts of variations: you can substitute almonds or cashews for the hazelnuts, use soy or rice milk instead of whole milk, or replace the honey with agave syrup. Experiment to find your favorite formula.*

CRUNCHY
ALMOND SPREAD

MAKES 2 CUPS

PREPARATION TIME 40 MINUTES

4¼ cups unblanched almonds
1½ cups sugar
3½ oz dark chocolate (70% cocoa)

STERILIZING THE JARS
Sterilize a 2-pint canning jar and lid by immersing it in boiling water for 3 minutes. Drain and dry on a rack before using.

MAKING THE ALMOND CARAMEL
Preheat the oven to 325°F. Place the almonds on a baking sheet and toast for 10 minutes. Remove from the oven and allow to cool. Put the sugar in a medium saucepan and follow the instructions on page 8 to make a light caramel. Add the almonds and stir to combine. Turn the mixture out onto a silicone mat and allow to cool completely.

MAKING THE SPREAD
Once the caramel is cool, break it into pieces and add to a food processor. Process until the mixture forms a coarse paste. Remove about 1 cup of the paste and set aside in a bowl. Continue to process the remaining paste until smooth. In a double boiler, melt the chocolate, add it to the food processor, and continue processing until well combined. Transfer to the bowl with the reserved paste and mix well. Spoon the spread into the prepared jar and seal. Store at room temperature for up to 2 weeks.

1920
~
1950

1761 ~ 1791

A SHOP WITH THE ALLURE OF A FARMHOUSE

1791 ~ 1807

THE FATE OF LE PÉRE DE FAMILLE

1807 ~ 1825

A FREE WOMAN

1825 ~ 1850

AT THE HEART OF ARTISTIC LIFE

1850 ~ 1895

A NEW ERA OF COOKIES

THE SOUL OF THE NEIGHBORHOOD

In the 1920s, the Rue du Faubourg-Montmartre is the turbulent artery for Paris nightlife thanks to its proximity to the Opéra, theatres, and conservatory for performing arts. The neighborhood marches to the beat of musicians and dancers. In this rowdy, artistic atmosphere, À la Mère de Famille stands as a guardian of tradition, and functions as the soul of the neighborhood. Its quaintness and nostalgic air makes it fashionable in a neighborhood that's better known for its wild nightlife. The store inspires writers, photographers, and then filmmakers; it supplies cabarets; and, after nightfall, the window displays bring back memories of childhood pleasures for night owls wandering by. All the while, Régis Dreux and his wife faithfully continue the work of Georges Lecœur. When Régis dies, in 1931, his only daughter and her husband—the Legrands—take over the establishment. They live close by, and Madame Legrand, who finds the cultural life of the neighborhood amusing, takes good care of the shop. Three years later, the couple adopts Suzanne, Madame Legrand's orphaned second cousin, who is twelve years old. With no children of their own, the Legrands teach Suzanne the trade. During World War II, the windows are whitewashed, but the store stays open to supply rations of chocolate and cookies. When the Liberation comes, the Legrands take back their business and, in 1946, recruit a new shop assistant, the young Albert Brethonneau. Albert and Suzanne fall in love working side by side at À la Mère de Famille.

In confectionery, the seasons and holidays influence production. Since the 1920s, the Easter displays at À la Mère de Famille have played host to numerous chocolate animals: fish and hens, as is customary, but also elephants, pelicans, and giraffes. In autumn, jams and candied fruit take pride of place. At Christmastime, truffles and *marrons glacés* make their long-awaited appearance in the store.

1895 ~ 1920
A CHILDHOOD DREAM COME TRUE

1920 ~ 1950
THE SOUL OF THE NEIGHBORHOOD

1950 ~ 1985
ALBERT AND SUZANNE

1985 ~ 2000
A TIME FOR CHOCOLATE

2000 ~
HISTORY IN THE MAKING

ORANGE MARMALADE

MAKES ABOUT **2** CUPS
PREPARATION TIME **1** HOUR
RESTING TIME OVERNIGHT
COOKING TIME **15** MINUTES

oranges 5
salt .... pinch
sugar ....4 cups per 2¼ lbs of fruit
cardamom seeds...4

PREPARING THE FRUIT

Wash the oranges and trim the ends off of each. Fill a large saucepan with water, add the salt, and bring to a boil over high heat. Immerse the oranges in the boiling water for 5 minutes, then drain. Repeat this process two more times using boiling unsalted water. Cool the oranges completely, then cut them into small cubes. Weigh the chopped oranges, transfer to a nonreactive large bowl, and add 4 cups sugar per 2½ lbs of fruit. Add the cardamom seeds, toss to combine, then cover with plastic wrap and leave to macerate overnight.

STERILIZING THE JARS

Sterilize three 4-ounce canning jars and lids by immersing them in boiling water for 3 minutes. Drain and dry on a rack before using.

COOKING THE FRUIT

The next day, transfer the oranges to a nonreactive saucepan, bring to a boil over high heat, and boil for 15 minutes. Remove from the heat, spoon the marmalade into the jars and seal. Store at room temperature for up to 2 months.

SIROP DE LIÈGE

MAKES ABOUT 2 CUPS

PREPARATION TIME 20 MINUTES
COOKING TIME 3 HOURS

7 pears
3 apples
1 cup water
¾ cup sugar

STERILIZING THE JAR
Sterilize an 8-ounce jar and lid by immersing them in boiling water for 3 minutes. Drain and dry on a rack before using.

PREPARING THE FRUIT
Wash the pears and apples and cut them into quarters, without removing the skin or the seeds.

MAKING THE JAM
Place the fruit and water in a large saucepan, cover, and bring to a simmer over low heat. Cook until the fruit has softened, then pour through a strainer lined with a double thickness of cheesecloth into a medium saucepan. Discard the solids. Add the sugar to the strained juice, bring to a simmer over low heat, and cook for 1 hour, stirring occasionally, until the mixture has the consistency of caramel. Immediately pour the jam into the jar and seal. Store in the refrigerator for up to 2 weeks.

HISTORY: *This apple and pear jam is a traditional Belgian preparation. It can be used as a spread and is sometimes added to flavor savory dishes, such as rabbit stew.*

MILK JAM

MAKES ABOUT 2 CUPS

COOKING TIME 1 HOUR

4 cups whole milk
2 cups sugar
2½ tbsp honey
1 vanilla bean, split lengthwise

STERILIZING THE JAR
Sterilize an 8-ounce jar and lid by immersing them in boiling water for 3 minutes. Drain and dry on a rack before using.

MAKING THE JAM
Combine the milk, sugar, and honey in a medium saucepan. Scrape the seeds from the vanilla bean into the pan and add the pod, then bring to a boil over high heat. Boil the mixture, stirring constantly, until it is the color of light caramel and thick enough to coat the back of a spoon, about 1 hour. Immediately spoon the jam into the jar and seal. Store at room temperature for up to 2 months. (After opening, refrigerate and use within 2 weeks.)

This rustic confection is actually a caramel sauce. It's delicious spread over a thick slice of bread or eaten right off a spoon!

RASPBERRY JAM

MAKES ABOUT 2 CUPS

PREPARATION TIME 10 MINUTES
MACERATING TIME 1 HOUR
COOKING TIME 20 MINUTES

1¼ lb raspberries
2 cups sugar

STERILIZING THE JARS
Sterilize two 8-ounce jars and lids by immersing them in boiling water for 3 minutes. Drain and dry on a rack before using.

MACERATING THE FRUIT
Wash the raspberries and place them in a medium heavy-bottomed saucepan. Add the sugar, toss to combine, then set aside for 1 hour.

MAKING THE JAM
Place the saucepan over medium-low heat and slowly bring to a boil, stirring occasionally and skimming the surface to remove any impurities. Increase the heat to medium-high and boil for about 15 minutes, until thickened. To check if the jam is ready, remove a small spoonful and allow it to cool slightly—it should be quite thick. If not, continue cooking and check again after a few minutes. When the jam has thickened, immediately spoon it into the jars and seal.

6

AN ARRAY OF BUTTERY SABLÉS, several types of almond cookies, tuiles, coconut macaroons, and plain and chocolate meringues are featured in this chapter. You'll think you've fallen into one of those cookie assortments carefully arranged in a large tin. Except that in this case, the cookies have the aroma of fresh butter and eggs, and are irresistably crisp and delicious. These recipes are must-haves in your culinary repertoire so you can proudly bring out homemade cookies at coffee time. They are revered, time-honored classics, and everyone is sure to find at least one to love!

BISCUITERIE

COOKIES, TUILES, AND MERINGUES

SABLÉS BRETON

MAKES ABOUT 30 COOKIES

PREPARATION TIME 10 MINUTES
RESTING TIME OVERNIGHT
BAKING TIME 15 MINUTES

3 egg yolks
¾ cup sugar
½ cup plus 2 tbsp unsalted butter, softened
1¾ cups all-purpose flour
1 tbsp baking powder
1 tsp salt

MAKING THE COOKIE DOUGH

In a large mixing bowl, whisk together the egg yolks and sugar until pale and thick. Beat in the butter until combined, then sift in the flour, baking powder, and salt. Stir the mixture until it forms a ball, wrap in plastic wrap, and refrigerate overnight.

BAKING

Adjust the oven racks to the upper- and lower-middle positions and preheat the oven to 325°F. Lightly grease thirty 2-inch pastry rings and place them on baking sheets lined with parchment paper. Roll out the dough to a ¼-inch thickness. Use one of the pastry rings to cut out circles of dough, then place one dough circle in each of the prepared rings on the baking sheets. Bake for 15 minutes, or until golden brown. Remove from the oven and cool on a wire rack. (Store the cookies in an airtight container for up to 2 weeks.)

BUTTER COOKIES

MAKES ABOUT 50 COOKIES

PREPARATION TIME 15 MINUTES
RESTING TIME 1 HOUR
BAKING TIME 20 MINUTES

1 cup plus 3 tbsp unsalted butter, softened
2 cups confectioners' sugar
2 eggs
4 cups all-purpose flour
A pinch of salt
Milk, for brushing

MAKING THE DOUGH

In a large mixing bowl, combine the butter and confectioners' sugar. Beat in the eggs, then sift in the flour and salt. Turn out the dough onto a large sheet of parchment paper, cover with a second sheet, and roll out to a thickness of $\frac{1}{16}$ to $\frac{1}{8}$ inch. Slide the parchment with the dough onto a baking sheet and refrigerate for 1 hour.

BAKING

Adjust the oven racks to the upper- and lower-middle positions and preheat the oven to 325°F. Remove the top sheet of parchment and use a 3-inch fluted round pastry cutter to cut out circles. Arrange the circles on baking sheets lined with parchment paper, spacing them about 1 inch apart. Use the tines of a fork to lightly create a striped effect on each cookie, then brush the tops with milk. Bake for about 20 minutes, until golden. Remove from the oven and cool on a wire rack. (Store the cookies in an airtight container for up to 1 week.)

VARIATION: *You can also try this recipe using salted butter.*

SPECULAAS

MAKES ABOUT 70 COOKIES

PREPARATION TIME 10 MINUTES
RESTING TIME 1 HOUR
BAKING TIME 15 MINUTES

½ cup plus 1 tbsp unsalted butter, softened
¾ cup packed dark brown sugar
1 egg
1¾ cups all-purpose flour
1 tbsp ground cinnamon
1 tsp baking powder

MAKING THE DOUGH

In a large mixing bowl, combine the butter and brown sugar. Mix in the egg, then sift in the flour, cinnamon, and baking powder and combine. Turn out the dough onto a large sheet of parchment paper, cover with a second sheet, and roll out to a thickness of ¹⁄₁₆ to ⅛ inch. Slide the parchment with the dough onto a baking sheet and refrigerate for 1 hour.

BAKING

Adjust the oven racks to the upper- and lower-middle positions and preheat the oven to 325°F. Remove the top sheet of parchment and cut the dough into 2-by-3-inch rectangles. Arrange the rectangles on baking sheets lined with parchment paper, spacing them about 1 inch apart. Bake for about 15 minutes, until they begin to brown at the edges. Remove from the oven and cool on a wire rack. (Store the cookies in an airtight container for up to 1 week.)

 CHEF'S TIP: *In France, the variety of sugar we use to make these traditional cookies is* vergeoise, *a very dark and moist sugar. American dark brown sugar and even muscovado sugar will work well in the recipe.*

ALMOND CROQUANTS

MAKES ABOUT 30 COOKIES

PREPARATION TIME 10 MINUTES
BAKING TIME 15 MINUTES

2 egg whites
1 cup plus 2 tbsp sugar
⅓ cup plus 1 tbsp all-purpose flour
1¼ cups sliced almonds

MAKING THE BATTER

In a large mixing bowl, combine the egg whites and sugar using a spatula. Sift in the flour. Finish by gently folding in the almonds, being careful not to break them.

BAKING

Adjust the oven racks to the upper- and lower-middle positions and preheat the oven to 375°F. Line two baking sheets with parchment paper. Using a tablespoon, drop mounds of batter onto the prepared baking sheets, spacing them about 2 inches apart. Bake for about 15 minutes, or until golden. Remove from the oven and allow the cookies to cool before removing from the baking sheets. (Store the cookies in an airtight container for up to 1 week.)

 CHEF'S TIP: *You can flavor these cookies with orange flower water or a little citrus zest.*

CUSTOMER PORTRAITS:
MARIE-ODILE CHAUVELOT

OCCUPATION . . . . Restaurateur
NEIGHBORHOOD . . . . .9th arrondissement
STORE VISITED . . . . .Rue du Faubourg-Montmartre
FIRST VISIT . . . . A very long time ago

FREQUENCY OF VISITS . . . . Once a month
FAVORITE CHOCOLATE . . . . .Dark
CHOCOLATE CONSUMPTION . Impossible to stop myself!

1
WHEN DO YOU VISIT THE STORE?
In the afternoon, after service.

2
WHAT IS YOUR GREATEST INDULGENCE?
The pavé de Tours.

3
YOUR GUILTY PLEASURE?
The palets Montmartre.

4
WHAT WAS YOUR CHILDHOOD TREAT?
Nougats and caramels.

5
WHAT KIND OF TREATS DO YOU LIKE TO SHARE?
Calissons.

6
THE TREAT YOU ENJOY ALONE?
The chocolate bars — Abinao or Manjari bean!

7
WHAT DO YOU THINK IS THE MOST ROMANTIC TREAT?
Marzipan cherries.

8
DO YOU HAVE A MEMORY CONNECTED TO THIS PLACE?
My whole childhood . . .

9
DESCRIBE A PERFECT MOMENT TIED TO A TREAT FROM À LA MÈRE DE FAMILLE.
Christmas and marrons glacés.

10
IF LA MÈRE WERE TO GIVE YOU A PRESENT, WHAT WOULD YOU LIKE IT TO BE?
A small box of chocolates.

11
WHAT DOES À LA MÈRE DE FAMILLE REPRESENT FOR YOU?
The perfect shop.

12
WHAT DO YOU THINK SHOULD BE THE MOTTO OF À LA MÈRE DE FAMILLE?
"You'll find everything here . . ."

13
WHAT IS THE SECRET TO ITS ENDURING SUCCESS?
Its respect for tradition.

14
WHAT MAKES THE SHOP DIFFERENT FROM THE OTHERS LIKE IT?
Its sincerity.

15
WHAT DOES THE STORE'S HISTORY EVOKE FOR YOU?
Authenticity and emotion.

ALMOND TUILES

MAKES ABOUT 40 TUILES

PREPARATION TIME 10 MINUTES
BAKING TIME 15 MINUTES

2 eggs
½ cup plus 2 tbsp sugar
3 tbsp all-purpose flour
1½ cups sliced almonds

MAKING THE BATTER

In a large mixing bowl, combine the eggs and sugar with a spatula. Sift in the flour, then gently fold in the almonds, being careful not to break them.

BAKING

Adjust the oven racks to the upper- and lower-middle positions and preheat the oven to 375°F. Line two baking sheets with parchment paper. Using a spoon, drop tablespoons of batter onto the prepared baking sheets, spacing them about 1 inch apart. Flatten each one with a fork to a round. Bake for about 10 minutes, or until the edges of the tuiles are deep golden brown.

SHAPING THE TUILES

As soon as the tuiles come out of the oven, while they are still hot, remove them one at a time from the baking sheets with a thin spatula and lay each one on a rolling pin or bottle to form a curved shape. Allow to cool completely. (Store the cookies in an airtight container away from moisture for up to 1 week.)

CHEF'S TIP: *To prevent the fork tines from sticking to the batter when you flatten the mounds, dip the fork in hot water to moisten. Tuiles take on a very interesting flavor if you add a little finely grated orange zest to the batter.*

HAZELNUT COOKIES

MAKES ABOUT 50 COOKIES

PREPARATION TIME 10 MINUTES
RESTING TIME 1 HOUR
BAKING TIME 12 MINUTES

½ cup plus 3 tbsp unsalted butter, softened
1⅓ cups confectioners' sugar
2 eggs
2¾ cups all-purpose flour
2½ tsp baking powder
1¼ cups hazelnuts, chopped

MAKING THE DOUGH

In a large mixing bowl, cream the butter and confectioners' sugar until pale. Add the eggs, one at a time, then sift in the flour and baking powder. Fold in the hazelnuts, then refrigerate the mixture.

BAKING

Adjust the oven racks to the upper- and lower-middle positions and preheat the oven to 375°F. Line two baking sheets with parchment paper. When the dough is firm, using your hands, roll the dough into a 10-inch-long cylinder, then flatten the cylinder so that it forms a long rectangle about 2 inches high. Using a sharp knife, cut the dough crosswise into ¼-inch-thick slices. Arrange the slices on the prepared baking sheets, spacing them about 1 inch apart. Bake for about 12 minutes, until golden. Remove from the oven and cool completely. (Store the cookies in an airtight container for up to 1 week.)

CHOCOLATE-PISTACHIO COOKIES

MAKES ABOUT 50 COOKIES

PREPARATION TIME 10 MINUTES
RESTING TIME 1 HOUR
BAKING TIME 12 MINUTES

1 cup unsalted butter, softened
¾ cup plus 2 tbsp confectioners' sugar
A pinch of salt
1 egg
6 tbsp unsweetened cocoa powder
2¼ cups all-purpose flour
¾ cup blanched pistachios

MAKING THE DOUGH

In a large mixing bowl, combine the butter, confectioners' sugar, and salt. Add the egg, then sift in the flour and cocoa and stir to combine. Fold in the pistachios, then, using your hands, roll the dough into a cylinder about 10 inches long and 2 inches in diameter. Then refrigerate the dough.

BAKING

Adjust the oven racks to the upper- and lower-middle positions and preheat the oven to 375°F. Line two baking sheets with parchment paper. When the dough is firm, use a sharp knife to cut the cylinder crosswise into ¼-inch-thick slices. Arrange the cookies on the prepared baking sheets, spacing them about 1 inch apart. Bake for about 12 minutes, until the tops appear dry. Remove from the oven and cool completely. (Store the cookies in an airtight container for up to 1 week.)

1950
~
1985

1761 ~ 1791

A SHOP WITH THE ALLURE OF A FARMHOUSE

1791 ~ 1807

THE FATE OF LE PÈRE DE FAMILLE

1807 ~ 1825

A FREE WOMAN

1825 ~ 1850

AT THE HEART OF ARTISTIC LIFE

1850 ~ 1895

A NEW ERA OF COOKIES

ALBERT AND SUZANNE

Albert and Suzanne to retire, they take great care in choosing their successor. Above all, they want to build on the store's reputation as a purveyor of high-quality chocolates, and this is why they choose Serge Neveu, one of the best artisan chocolatiers in France, who has already been charmed by the boutique and its sweets. He makes his passion for chocolate one of the *raisons d'être* of À la Mère de Famille.

In 1950, Albert and Suzanne married. Over time, À La Mère de Famille becomes the story of their life.

It's with a very special affection that the couple decides to carry on the tradition when the Legrands hand the shop over to them. Under Suzanne and Albert, À la Mère de Famille remains a Parisian landmark. Most of the goodies offered at the beginning of the century by Georges Lecœur are still sold: chocolates, confectionery from all over France, dried fruit and nuts, cakes, the famous Plum Plouvier babas, Breton fruits preserved in eau-de-vie, marrons glacés, and twenty-five kinds of petits fours. Suzanne becomes famous for her elaborate store displays, and her beautiful seasonal window arrangements impress all who stroll past. À la Mère de Famille becomes a celebrated source for chocolates; Parisians refer to the Brethonneaus as the new chocolatiers of Paris. When the time comes for

À la Mère de Famille has undergone many changes over the years, but preserving the look, feel, and spirit of the original shop has always been a concern. In 1984, this unique establishment was listed as one of Paris's *monuments historiques*.

1895 ~ 1920	1920 ~ 1950	1950 ~ 1985	1985 ~ 2000	2000 ~
A CHILDHOOD DREAM COME TRUE	THE SOUL OF THE NEIGHBORHOOD	ALBERT AND SUZANNE	A TIME FOR CHOCOLATE	HISTORY IN THE MAKING

MONTPENSIER

MAKES TEN **3**-INCH CAKES
PREPARATION TIME **10** MINUTES
BAKING TIME **15** MINUTES

confectioners' sugar .... 2½ cups
ground almonds or almond meal.. 1¾ cups
all-purpose flour .... ¾ cup plus 2 tbsp
eggs.. 5
unsalted butter, melted... 3½ tbsp
salt .... pinch
sliced almonds... ½ cup

MAKING THE BATTER

In a large mixing bowl, combine the confectioners' sugar and ground almonds. Sift in the flour, stir to combine, then add 3 of the eggs. Separate the remaining 2 eggs, adding the yolks to the almond mixture and placing the whites in a clean, dry medium mixing bowl. Add the melted butter to the mixture and stir to combine. Whip the egg whites with the salt until they hold soft peaks. Gently fold the egg whites into the almond mixture.

BAKING

Preheat the oven to 325°F. Lightly grease ten 3-inch round cake pans and scatter the bottom of each with some sliced almonds. Divide the batter evenly among the prepared pans and bake for 15 minutes, until golden. Remove from the oven, turn the cakes out of the pans, and allow to cool completely on a wire rack. (Store in an airtight container for up to 3 days.)

PETITE MERINGUES

MAKES ABOUT 50 MERINGUES

PREPARATION TIME 15 MINUTES
BAKING TIME 4 HOURS

3 egg whites
7 tbsp granulated sugar
1 cup confectioners' sugar

MAKING THE MERINGUE

Place the egg whites and granulated sugar in the bowl of a stand mixer. Fill a saucepan with an inch of water, set it over medium heat, then position the bowl on the saucepan. Heat the mixture, whisking constantly, until it registers about 115°F on an instant-read thermometer. Fit the bowl on the mixer and whip with the whisk attachment on high speed until the meringue is fluffy, voluminous, and cool to the touch, about 8 minutes. Sift the confectioners' sugar over the meringue and fold it in with a spatula.

BAKING

Adjust the oven racks to upper- and lower-middle positions and preheat the oven to 200°F. Line two baking sheets with parchment paper. If using a piping bag, fit it with a ½-inch star tip. Fill the piping bag with the meringue and pipe 1-inch stars onto the prepared baking sheets. Alternatively, use a spoon to make neat dollops. Bake for 4 hours or more, depending on the size of the meringues, until completely crisp and dry inside. (Store in an airtight container for up to 2 days.)

CHEF'S TIP: *Meringues dry out in the oven rather than bake, so the process is very long and gentle. Meringues can be subtly flavored—try adding one or two drops of rose water, for example.*

COCONUT MACAROONS

MAKES ABOUT 40 MACAROONS

PREPARATION TIME 15 MINUTES
RESTING TIME 2 HOURS
BAKING TIME 4 MINUTES

3 egg whites
1 cup plus 2 tbsp sugar
2½ cups unsweetened shredded coconut

MAKING THE BATTER

Place the egg whites and sugar in the bowl of a stand mixer. Fill a saucepan with an inch of water, set it over medium heat, then position the bowl on the saucepan. Heat the mixture, whisking constantly, until it registers about 115°F on an instant-read thermometer. Fit the bowl on the mixer and whip with the whisk attachment on high speed until the mixture is fluffy, voluminous, and cool to the touch, about 10 minutes. Using a spatula, fold in the coconut.

BAKING

Line two baking sheets with parchment paper. Use a spoon to drop tablespoon-size mounds of batter onto the baking sheets. Set aside to dry for 2 hours at room temperature. Preheat the oven to 450°F. Bake the macaroons, one tray at a time, for 4 minutes, until lightly browned. (Store in an airtight container for up to 2 days.)

MAMIE JOJO'S MERINGUES

MAKES 10 MERINGUES

PREPARATION TIME 20 MINUTES
BAKING TIME 4 HOURS

FOR THE MERINGUE
3 egg whites
7 tbsp granulated sugar
¾ cup confectioners' sugar

FOR THE CHOCOLATE GANACHE
1 cup whipping cream
1 tbsp honey
6 oz dark chocolate (70% cocoa), chopped
4½ tbsp unsalted butter, softened
Unsweetened cocoa powder, for dusting

MAKING THE MERINGUE

Adjust the oven rack to the upper- and lower-middle positions and preheat the oven to 200°F. Line two baking sheets with parchment paper. Place the egg whites and granulated sugar in the bowl of an electric mixer. Fill a saucepan with an inch of water, set it over medium heat, then position the bowl on the saucepan. Heat the mixture, whisking constantly, until it registers 115°F on an instant-read thermometer. Fit the bowl on the mixer and whip with the whisk attachment at high speed until the meringue is fluffy, voluminous, and cool to the touch, about 10 minutes. Sift the confectioners' sugar over the meringue and fold it in with a spatula. Using a spoon, form twenty 3-inch rounds on the prepared baking sheets. Bake for 4 hours, until the meringues are crisp and dry.

MAKING THE GANACHE

In a medium saucepan, warm the cream and honey over medium heat to just under the boiling point. Put the chocolate in a medium mixing bowl and pour the hot cream over it. Gently stir with a spatula until smooth. When the mixture registers 95°F on the thermometer, stir in the butter. Set aside for 2 hours at room temperature to set.

ASSEMBLY

Spread about 2 tbsp ganache on the bottom side of one meringue and sandwich the ganache with another meringue. Repeat with the remaining meringues and ganache. Dust with cocoa powder. (Store in an airtight container for up to 2 days.)

ALMOND MACARONS

MAKES ABOUT 50 MACARONS

PREPARATION TIME 20 MINUTES
RESTING TIME 15 MINUTES
BAKING TIME 12 MINUTES

FOR THE MACARON BATTER
4 cups ground almonds or almond meal
2¾ cups plus 2 tbsp sugar
6 egg whites
½ cup water

FOR THE FILLING
1 cup raspberry jam (page 208) or chocolate ganache (page 236)

MAKING THE MACARON BATTER

Place the ground almonds, 1 cup plus 2 tbsp of the sugar, and 4 of the egg whites in a food processor and process for 4 minutes to make a smooth paste. Leave the mixture in the food processor. In a medium saucepan, combine 1½ cups plus 2 tbsp of the remaining sugar and the water and cook over high heat until the syrup registers 245°F on a candy thermometer. Meanwhile, in a clean, dry, medium mixing bowl, whip the remaining 2 egg whites and 2 tbsp sugar to stiff peaks. Pour the hot sugar syrup over the almond mixture in the food processor and process to combine. Tranfer to a large bowl, then fold in the beaten egg whites with a spatula.

BAKING

Adjust the oven racks to the upper- and lower-middle positions and preheat the oven to 400°F. Line two baking sheets with parchment paper. Fit a piping bag with a ¼-inch plain tip. Fill the piping bag with the batter and pipe 1½-inch circles onto the prepared baking sheets, spacing them about 1 inch apart. Leave to dry for 15 minutes at room temperature, then bake the macarons for about 12 minutes, until dry. Remove from the oven, let set for 5 minutes, then detach from the parchment and let cool completely.

ASSEMBLY

Spread some raspberry jam or chocolate ganache on the bottom side of one macaron and sandwich the filling with another macaron. Repeat with the remaining macarons and filling. Store in an airtight container for up to 2 days.

PUITS D'AMOUR

MAKES ABOUT 15 COOKIES

PREPARATION TIME 15 MINUTES
RESTING TIME 1 HOUR
BAKING TIME 15 MINUTES

FOR THE DOUGH
½ cup unsalted butter, softened
¾ cup confectioners' sugar, plus more for dusting
1 tsp salt
⅓ cup ground almonds
1 egg
2 cups all-purpose flour

FOR THE FILLING
1 cup raspberry jam (page 208)

MAKING THE DOUGH
In a large mixing bowl, combine the butter, confectioners' sugar, and salt. Add the ground almonds. Mix in the egg, then sift in the flour and mix well. Turn out the dough onto a large sheet of parchment paper, cover with a second sheet, and roll out to a thickness of ¹⁄₁₆ inch. Slide the parchment with the dough onto a baking sheet and refrigerate for 1 hour.

CUTTING THE DOUGH
Line two baking sheets with parchment paper. Cut out shapes from the dough using a 2-inch-long fluted oval-shaped pastry cutter and arrange on the prepared baking sheets. Use a ¾-inch round pastry cutter or a sharp knife to cut out two circles in the center of half of the ovals.

BAKING
Adjust the oven racks to the upper- and lower-middle positions and preheat the oven to 325°F. Bake the cookies for about 15 minutes, until golden. Remove from the oven and cool completely. Spread each of the cookies without holes with raspberry jam. Top each with a cookie with holes. Dust with confectioners' sugar. (Store in an airtight container for up to 1 week.)

HISTORY: *The classic name for these cookies is* lunettes *(French for "eyeglasses"), but Mamie Jojo called them* puits d'amour, *or "wells of love."*

MACARONS DE NANCY

MAKES ABOUT 50 MACARONS

PREPARATION TIME 10 MINUTES
BAKING TIME 15 MINUTES

1¾ cups confectioners' sugar, plus more as needed
2 cups ground almonds or almond meal, plus more as needed
3 egg whites, plus more as needed

MAKING THE BATTER

Put all of the ingredients in a large mixing bowl and mix with a whisk to combine. The batter should be firm enough to hold its shape, with a smooth surface. If it is too firm, add an additional egg white. If it is too soft, add more sugar and almonds, in equal amounts.

BAKING

Adjust the oven racks to the upper- and lower-middle positions and preheat the oven to 350°F. Line two baking sheets with parchment paper. Fit a piping bag with a ½-inch plain tip. Fill the piping bag with the batter and pipe 1-inch mounds of batter onto the prepared baking sheets. Tap the baking sheets to smooth the surface of the mounds. Dust the tops with confectioners' sugar, then spray with water until lightly dampened. Bake for about 15 minutes. Remove from the oven and cool completely. (Store in an airtight container for up to 1 week.)

HISTORY: *This recipe is for the traditional* macaron, *plain and simple, not the fashion victim that is the Parisian* macaron.

7

À LA MÈRE DE FAMILLE

also offers artisanal ice creams in wonderfully original flavors such as black sesame and rose praline. This chapter holds secrets that will allow you to produce frozen treats at home that are irresistably unique and deliciously diabolical! Chocolate-coated ice pops and made-to-order sundaes combine the intense creaminess of classic ice cream with the crispest of confections or the most luscious of sauces. Consider yourself warned!

FROZEN TREATS

EXOTIC ICE POPS
WITH GIANDUJA COOKIES

MAKES ABOUT 15 ICE POPS

PREPARATION TIME 1 HOUR 15 MINUTES
FREEZING TIME OVERNIGHT

FOR THE COOKIES
7 oz puits d'amour cookie dough (page 240)
3 oz gianduja (hazelnut chocolate), chopped
¾ oz dark chocolate (70% cocoa), chopped

FOR THE COATING
14 oz dark chocolate (70% cocoa), chopped
3 tbsp sunflower oil
½ cup chopped toasted hazelnuts

FOR THE SORBET
⅔ cup water
1 cup plus 2 tbsp sugar
1 tbsp honey
2 cups mango or passion fruit purée

MAKING THE COOKIES
Preheat the oven to 325°F. Line a baking sheet with parchment paper. Roll out the dough to a thickness of ⅛ inch (the shape doesn't matter) and bake on the prepared baking sheet for about 20 minutes. Allow to cool, then crumble the cookie into a bowl. In a double boiler, melt together the gianduja and dark chocolate. Add the crumbled cookie, stir to combine, then spread the mixture into a ¼-inch-thick layer on a sheet of parchment. Refrigerate until set, about 30 minutes, then cut into ¼-inch cubes.

MAKING THE SORBET BASE
Put the water, sugar, and honey in a saucepan and bring to a boil. In a medium bowl, stir together the sugar syrup and the fruit purée. Cover and refrigerate until chilled.

FREEZING THE ICE POPS
Churn the sorbet base in an ice-cream machine according to the manufacturer's instructions. Once it is semifirm, stir in the chocolate-covered cookie pieces. Using a piping bag fitted with a large plain tip, pipe the mixture into ice-pop molds and insert a wooden stick into each. Freeze overnight.

COATING THE ICE POPS
In a double boiler, heat the dark chocolate until it is melted and registers 95°F on an instant-read thermometer. Add the sunflower oil and hazelnuts and stir to combine. Remove the ice pops from the molds. Quickly dip each ice pop in the chocolate to coat, then wait for the chocolate to completely set before laying the ice pop down. Return to the freezer or enjoy straight away!

CHOCOLATE-CARAMEL ICE POPS

MAKES ABOUT 15 ICE POPS

PREPARATION TIME 1 HOUR 15 MINUTES
FREEZING TIME OVERNIGHT

FOR THE ICE-CREAM BASE
2½ cups whole milk
3 tbsp milk powder
½ cup whipping cream
½ cup sugar
2 tbsp honey
110 g dark chocolate (70% cocoa), chopped

FOR THE CARAMEL
½ cup whipping cream
½ cup sugar
3½ tbsp unsalted butter
A pinch of salt

¾ cup folies de l'écureuil (page 85), chopped

FOR THE COATING
14 oz dark chocolate (70% cocoa)
3 tbsp sunflower oil
1¼ cups chopped toasted almonds

MAKING THE ICE-CREAM BASE

Put the milk in a medium saucepan and heat over medium heat until warm, then add the milk powder, cream, sugar, honey, and chocolate. When the mixture registers 180°F on an instant-read thermometer, transfer to a blender and blend for 1 minute. Transfer to a container, cover, and refrigerate until chilled.

MAKING THE CARAMEL

In a small saucepan, warm the cream over medium heat. Put the sugar in a medium saucepan and follow the instructions on page 8 to make a light caramel. Add the warm cream and continue to cook until the caramel registers 220°F. Stir in the butter and salt, transfer to a blender, and blend until smooth. Refrigerate until chilled.

FREEZING THE ICE POPS

Churn the ice-cream base in an ice-cream machine according to the manufacturer's instructions. Once it is semifirm, add the folies de l'écureuil and caramel and use a spatula to create a swirled effect. Using a piping bag fitted with a large plain tip, pipe the ice cream into ice-pop molds and insert a wooden stick into each. Freeze overnight.

COATING THE ICE POPS

In a double boiler, heat the chocolate until it is melted and registers 95°F. Add the sunflower oil and almonds and stir to combine. Remove the ice pops from the molds. Quickly dip each ice pop in the chocolate to coat, then wait for the chocolate to completely set before laying the ice pop down. Return to the freezer or enjoy straight away!

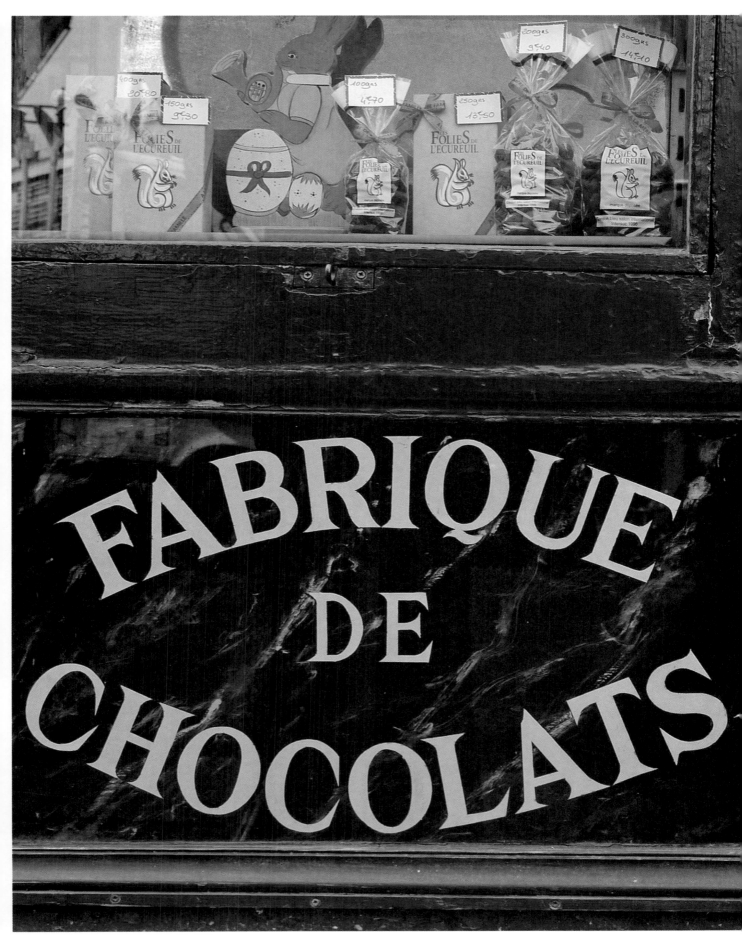

Crunchy popsicles!

PISTACHIO ICE POPS

MAKES ABOUT 15 ICE POPS

PREPARATION TIME 1 HOUR 15 MINUTES
FREEZING TIME OVERNIGHT

FOR THE PISTACHIO ICE-CREAM
2½ cups milk
3½ tbsp milk powder
3½ tbsp whipping cream
¾ cup sugar
1 tbsp honey
3 egg yolks
3½ oz pistachio paste (page 160)
2½ oz calissons (page 162), chopped
¼ cup pistachios, chopped

FOR THE COATING
14 oz milk chocolate, chopped
3 tbsp sunflower oil
Chopped toasted pistachios

MAKING THE ICE-CREAM BASE

Pour the milk into a medium saucepan and warm over medium heat until it registers 105°F on an instant-read thermometer. Add the milk powder, cream, sugar, honey, egg yolks, and pistachio paste. Continue to cook, stirring constantly, until the mixture registers 180°F. Strain into a blender and blend for 1 minute to smooth and aerate the mixture. Cover and refrigerate until chilled.

FREEZING THE ICE POPS

Churn the ice-cream base in an ice-cream machine according to the manufacturer's instructions. Once it is semifirm, fold in the calissons and pistachios. Using a piping bag fitted with a large plain tip, pipe the ice cream into ice-pop molds and insert a wooden stick into each. Freeze overnight.

COATING THE ICE POPS

In a double boiler, heat the chocolate until it is melted and registers 95°F. Add the sunflower oil and and stir to combine. Remove the ice pops from the molds. Quickly dip each ice pop in the chocolate to coat, then sprinkle with chopped pistachios. Wait for the chocolate to completely set before laying the ice pops down. Return to the freezer or enjoy straight away!

 EQUIPMENT: *Ice pop molds in various kid-pleasing shapes are readily available in housewares stores.*

RASPBERRY ICE POPS
WITH BURSTS OF PÂTE DE FRUITS

MAKES ABOUT 15 ICE POPS

PREPARATION TIME 1 HOUR 15 MINUTES
FREEZING TIME OVERNIGHT

FOR THE RASPBERRY SORBET
½ cup water
1 cup sugar
1½ tbsp honey
1⅓ lbs raspberries, puréed
3½ oz raspberry pâte de fruits
(see variation, page 168), diced

FOR THE COATING
14 oz dark chocolate (70% cocoa), chopped
3 tbsp sunflower oil
Chopped toasted hazelnuts

MAKING THE SORBET BASE

In a large saucepan, combine the water, sugar, and honey and bring to a boil over high heat. Place the raspberry purée in a bowl and pour the sugar syrup over it. Cover and refrigerate until chilled.

FREEZING THE ICE POPS

Churn the sorbet base in an ice-cream machine according to the manufacturer's instructions. Once it is semifirm, fold in the pâte de fruits. Using a piping bag fitted with a large plain tip, pipe the sorbet into ice-pop molds and insert a wooden stick into each. Freeze overnight.

COATING THE ICE POPS

In a double boiler, heat the chocolate until it is melted and registers 95°F on an instant-read thermometer. Add the sunflower oil and stir to combine. Remove the ice pops from the molds. Quickly dip each ice pop in the chocolate to coat, then sprinkle with chopped hazelnuts. Wait for the chocolate to completely set before laying the ice pops down. Return to the freezer or enjoy straight away!

VARIATION: *If you don't have time to make ice pops, this sorbet is delicious on its own!*

Raspberry

Pistachio

1985 ~ 2000

1761 ~ 1791

A SHOP WITH THE ALLURE OF A FARMHOUSE

1791 ~ 1807

THE FATE OF LE PÈRE DE FAMILLE

1807 ~ 1825

A FREE WOMAN

1825 ~ 1850

AT THE HEART OF ARTISTIC LIFE

1850 ~ 1895

A NEW ERA OF COOKIES

A TIME FOR CHOCOLATE

Renowned pâtissier and chocolatier Serge Neveu takes over À la Mère de Famille in the 1980s.

His wife and daughter, also under the spell of this timeless store, run the business by his side. The workshop once used for making preserves is turned into a chocolate laboratory and, for the first time in the shop's history, Serge Neveu begins manufacturing chocolates in-house. His creations take their place in the display windows, alongside seasonal specialities. In the great À la Mère de Famille tradition, Serge Neveu and his wife decorate the window for festive occasions: Valentine's Day, Easter, Mother's Day, Christmas. The now-famous chocolatier develops special chocolates for each. In 1989, the Paris Chamber of Commerce and Industry awards him the prestigious Nef d'Or in recognition of his work. More than two hundred years after it first opened, À la Mère de Famille is more than ever a destination for Parisian gourmands and tourists from all over the world who are fascinated by this unique establishment. By the early 1990s, Serge Neveu surrounds himself with the best artisans and suppliers, and offers an incredible menu of sweet treats: pralines, *pâtes de fruits*, *marrons glacés*, chocolate-covered almonds and hazelnuts, chocolate "olives," nougats, and candied fruits.

The Théâtre Trévise, Théâtre Mogador, Théâtre de Paris, Théâtre du Nord-Ouest, Théâtre des Nouveautés, and Splendid are all within walking distance to À la Mère de Famille. It's no surprise that many great actors come between rehearsals to buy their sweets at the shop.

1895 ~ 1920	1920 ~ 1950	1950 ~ 1985	1985 ~ 2000	2000 ~
A CHILDHOOD DREAM COME TRUE	THE SOUL OF THE NEIGHBORHOOD	ALBERT AND SUZANNE	A TIME FOR CHOCOLATE	HISTORY IN THE MAKING

PLAIN CAKE
WITH CANDIED ORANGE

SERVES 8
PREPARATION TIME 20 MINUTES
BAKING TIME 40 MINUTES

eggs...8
sugar ....1¼ cups
all-purpose flour .... 2 cups
unsalted butter, melted.. ½ cup plus 1 tbsp
candied orange peel (page 102), finely chopped ....1½ cups

MAKING THE BATTER

Separate 5 of the eggs, adding the yolks to a large mixing bowl; reserve the whites in a clean, dry medium mixing bowl. Add the sugar to the yolks and whisk until pale in color. Add the flour and the 3 remaining whole eggs. Incorporate the melted butter. Add the candied orange peel and stir to combine. Whip the reserved egg whites to firm peaks and gently fold them into the batter using a spatula.

BAKING THE CAKE

Preheat the oven to 325°F. Lightly grease a 10-inch round cake pan. Pour the batter into the prepared pan and bake for about 40 minutes, or until the blade of a knife comes out clean when inserted into the center of the cake. Remove from the oven, turn the cake out of the pan, and allow to cool. Serve at room temperature, or store in an airtight container for up to 1 week.

ICE CREAM SUNDAES

MAKES 10 SMALL SUNDAES

PREPARATION TIME 1 HOUR
RESTING TIME 1 NIGHT

2 cups whole milk
2 vanilla beans, split lengthwise
3 tbsp milk powder
¼ cup whipping cream
1 cup sugar
4 egg yolks
Choice of toppings (see page 262)

MAKING THE ICE-CREAM BASE

Put the milk in a medium saucepan, scrape the seeds from the vanilla beans, and add both the seeds and the pods to the pan. Bring to just under a boil over medium-high heat, then remove from the heat and set aside to infuse for 1 hour. Whisk in the milk powder, cream, sugar, and egg yolks. Place the pan over medium heat and cook, stirring constantly, until the mixture reaches 180°F on an instant-read thermometer. Strain the mixture through a fine-mesh sieve into a bowl and discard the vanilla pods. Transfer to a blender and blend for 1 minute to aerate the mixture, then refrigerate until chilled.

ASSEMBLING THE SUNDAES

Churn the ice-cream base in an ice-cream machine according to the manufacturer's instructions. Place ten small glass bowls or cups in the freezer for 20 minutes to chill. Fit a piping bag with a large fluted nozzle with the ice cream. Pipe ice cream into the chilled bowls and add the topping of your choice. Serve immediately.

 EQUIPMENT: *If you don't have an ice-cream machine, buy good-quality ice cream and embellish it with your favorite toppings on page 262.*

SUNDAE TOPPINGS

CARAMEL SAUCE

½ cup sugar
½ cup whipping cream, warmed
3½ tbsp unsalted butter
A pinch of salt

Put the sugar in a medium saucepan and follow the instructions on page 8 to make a light caramel. Add the warm cream to the caramel and continue cooking until it registers 220°F on a candy thermometer. Add the butter and salt and stir until well combined. Let cool, then refrigerate until ready to serve.

CARAMELIZED ALMONDS

2 tbsp water
2 tbsp sugar
1¼ cups slivered almonds

Preheat the oven to 325°F. Combine the water and sugar in a medium saucepan and cook over medium heat, stirring until the sugar dissolves. Add the almonds and stir to coat. Pour the mixture onto a small baking sheet and toast in the oven, stirring regularly, until caramelized, about 10 minutes.

FRUIT COULIS

½ cup fresh fruit purée
1 tbsp sugar
1½ tsp honey

Place all of the ingredients in a blender and blend until smooth. Refrigerate until ready to serve.

8

WHEN HOT WEATHER comes, nothing impresses a crowd more than bringing out a little homemade syrup to flavor a tall drink made with cold seltzer and a few ice cubes. Naturally and deliciously flavored, yet utterly simple! In this chapter is a short selection of our favorites: lemon-lime, strawberry (but with *spices*), grenadine (made with real pomegranates), and fresh mint. They are all classics with a twist!

RECIPES FOR SYRUPS

LEMON-LIME SYRUP

PREPARATION TIME 15 MINUTES
COOKING TIME 3 MINUTES
STEEPING TIME OVERNIGHT

2¼ cups sugar
4 lemons
2 limes
½ cup water

MAKING THE SYRUP

Add the sugar to a medium nonreactive saucepan, and finely grate the zest from the lemons and limes over the top. Squeeze the juice from all the fruit into the pan. Add the water, bring to a boil, remove from the heat, and allow the syrup to steep overnight at room temperature.

STERILIZING THE BOTTLE

Sterilize a clean 750-ml glass bottle by immersing it in boiling water for 3 minutes. Drain and dry on a rack before using.

BOTTLING THE SYRUP

Strain the syrup through a fine-mesh sieve into a clean nonreactive saucepan. Bring the syrup to a boil over high heat and cook for 3 minutes, then pour it into the sterilized bottle. Refrigerate for up to 1 month. (To serve, allow one part syrup to five parts water.)

If you don't have a fine-mesh sieve, place one or two pieces of fine cheesecloth or a clean cotton napkin in a regular strainer to filter the syrup.

SPICED STRAWBERRY SYRUP

MAKES ONE 750-ML BOTTLE

PREPARATION TIME 10 MINUTES
COOKING TIME 3 MINUTES
INFUSION TIME OVERNIGHT

1 lb strawberries
2¼ cups sugar
3 star anise pods
1 cinnamon stick
½ vanilla bean, split lengthwise

MAKING THE SYRUP
Wash and hull the strawberries. Place in a blender with the sugar and purée. Transfer to a bowl, add the star anise and cinnamon stick, and scrape in the seeds from the vanilla bean. Cover and refrigerate overnight to allow the flavors to infuse.

STERILIZING THE BOTTLE
Sterlize a clean 750-ml glass bottle by immersing it in boiling water for 3 minutes. Drain and dry on a rack before using.

BOTTLING THE SYRUP
Strain the syrup through a fine-mesh sieve into a clean saucepan. Bring the syrup to a boil and cook for 3 minutes, then pour it into the sterilized bottle. Refrigerate for up to 1 month. (To serve, allow one part syrup to five parts water.)

You can, of course, make this syrup without the spices if you prefer. You can also combine strawberries and raspberries for a different berry flavor.

GRENADINE

MAKES ONE 750-ML BOTTLE

PREPARATION TIME 20 MINUTES
COOKING TIME 3 MINUTES
MACERATING TIME 1 HOUR

2¼ lbs pomegranates
Sugar

MAKING THE SYRUP
Cut the pomegranates in half and scoop the seeds into a mixing bowl. Add ½ cup sugar, let macerate for 1 hour, then purée in a blender. Strain the mixture through a fine-mesh sieve and weigh it. Pour the juice into a medium saucepan and add the same weight in sugar. Bring to a boil over high heat, stirring occasionally, and cook for 3 minutes, then skim the surface to remove any impurities.

STERILIZING THE BOTTLE
Sterilize a clean 750-ml glass bottle by immersing it in boiling water for 3 minutes. Drain and dry on a rack before using.

BOTTLING THE SYRUP
Pour the syrup into the sterilized bottle. Refrigerate for up to 1 month. (To serve, allow one part syrup to five parts water.)

 Grenadine is delicious stirred into a glass of sparkling water or used to flavor cocktails. A more clever option is to use it sparingly in certain savory dishes, such as in a sauce for seared foie gras or in a salad dressing.

MINT SYRUP

MAKES 1¾ CUPS

PREPARATION TIME 15 MINUTES
INFUSION TIME OVERNIGHT

30 mint sprigs
1¼ cups water
2 cups sugar

MAKING THE SYRUP

Wash the mint leaves, removing any stems. In a medium saucepan, combine the water, sugar, and mint leaves. Bring to a boil over high heat, then immediately remove from the heat. Let cool and refrigerate overnight to allow the flavor to infuse.

STERILIZING THE BOTTLE

Sterlize a clean 750-ml glass bottle by immersing it in boiling water for 3 minutes. Drain and dry on a rack before using.

BOTTLING THE SYRUP

Strain the mixture through a fine-mesh sieve into a clean saucepan. Bring to a boil over high heat and cook for 3 minutes, then pour the syrup into the sterilized bottle. Refrigerate for up to 1 month. (To serve, allow one part syrup to five parts water.)

2000

~

...

1761 ~ 1791

A SHOP WITH THE ALLURE OF A FARMHOUSE

1791 ~ 1807

THE FATE OF LE PÈRE DE FAMILLE

1807 ~ 1825

A FREE WOMAN

1825 ~ 1850

AT THE HEART OF ARTISTIC LIFE

1850 ~ 1895

A NEW ERA OF COOKIES

HISTORY IN THE MAKING

The succession of Serge Neveu is yet another affair of the heart. The Dolfi family—Étienne and his three children, Sophie, Jane, and Steve—takes over the store, all of them having fallen under the spell of À la Mère de Famille. Like Georges Lecœur in his time, the Dolfis bring something new by creating a website, opening other branches in Paris, inhabiting a corner in the Printemps department store on Boulevard Haussmann, and adding new sweet treats to the mix. As always, the Easter and Christmas creations are anticipated each season, and in the meantime, the many new, delicious, and amusing surprises become the talk of the town. The evolution of À la Mère de Famille combines its legendary history with a contemporary perspective. Today, Julien Merceron—pâtissier, chocolatier, ice-cream maker, and confectioner—brings his own know-how and innovation. The one-man-force behind 33, a laboratory located next door to the 9th arrondissement store, Merceron works with a master craftsman (a *Meilleur Ouvrier de France*, no less) as he plays with the shop's traditional confections (calissons, candied fruits, marshmallows) and then uses them as inspiration for his original creations. By its 250th birthday, what began in the eighteenth century as a little grocery store had become a place of legend, with a decor from another time but with an array of delights full of rejuvenated flavor. Chocolates, caramels, *pâtes de fruits*, ice creams, lollipops, marzipan, nougats, and, of course, *marrons glacés*—all are recognized as the best in Paris.

The 33 laboratory was created so that Merceron could give full expression to his creativity. This unique place adjoining the historic Faubourg-Montmartre store opens onto the street so that passers-by can share in the delicious experiments before they are sold next door. There are always so many new creations to discover—and savor—at À la Mère de Famille.

1895 ~ 1920
A CHILDHOOD DREAM COME TRUE

1920 ~ 1950
THE SOUL OF THE NEIGHBORHOOD

1950 ~ 1985
ALBERT AND SUZANNE

1985 ~ 2000
A TIME FOR CHOCOLATE

2000 ~
HISTORY IN THE MAKING
*

À LA MÈRE DE FAMILLE

Maison fondée en 1761

MAGASIN SPÉCIAL DE DESSERTS D'HIVER

G. LECŒUR

3̵7̵, Faubourg Montmartre et 1, Rue de Provence

Téléphone : Gutenberg 25-46

APPENDICES

IV

CANDIED FRUITS AND SUCH

V

JAMS AND SPREADS

CUSTOMER PORTRAITS

VI

COOKIES, TUILES, AND MERINGUES

VII

FROZEN TREATS

VIII

RECIPES FOR SYRUPS

ACKNOWLEDGMENTS

We would like to especially thank Jean-Marc, without whom
À la Mère de Famille would not be what it is today.

We would also like to thank:
Rosemarie, for her experience, initiative, and advice.
Jean for his inspiration, sensitivity, and his excellence as a photographer.
Pauline for her talent, humor, and patience.
Sophie and Julie for their magnificent and peerless drawing skills.
Lene for her calm under all circumstances.
Our in-house supermodels: Colette, Sophie, Georgette, Marie,
Stéphane, and Thomas.
Pauline, Fanny, and Marie-Laure for their keen eye!
Keda for her kind advice about the recipes.
Callist, who helped us to trace the wonderful history of À la Mère de
Famille.
Benoît and Ivan for the elegance of their designs, and Tao for his readiness
to listen and adapt.
Dominique Dufor for his spontaneous and generous help.
Serge Neveu who believed in us and entrusted us with his baby.

To all of our colleagues at À la Mère de Famille, thanks to you, with each
passing day it becomes more and more beautiful.

We dedicate this book to all of the customers of À La Mère de Famille.
It is because of you that the adventure continues!

À LA MÈRE DE FAMILLE LOCATIONS

Paris 9th: 35 Rue du Faubourg-Montmartre, tel. 01 47 70 83 69
Paris 6th: 39 Rue du Cherche-Midi, tel. 01 42 22 49 99
Paris 7th: 47 Rue Cler, tel. 01 45 55 29 74
Paris 16th: 59 Rue de la Pompe, tel. 01 45 04 73 19
Paris 17th: 30 Rue Legendre, tel. 01 47 63 52 94
Paris 17th: 107 Rue Jouffroy d'Abbans, tel. 01 47 63 15 15
Saint-Maur - 94100: 7 Avenue Charles de Gaulle,
tel. 01 42 83 81 49
Paris 2nd: 82 Rue Montorgueil, tel. 01 53 40 82 78
Printemps Haussman, Paris 9th: 64 Boulevard Haussmann,
tel. 01 42 82 49 56

To help you make the recipes in this book, you can find a selection of
ingredients and tools on our site:
www.lameredefamille.com

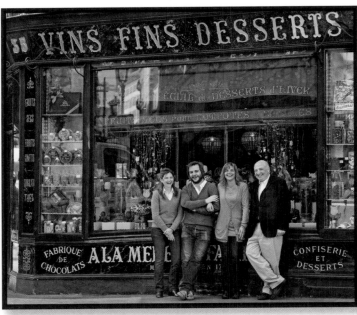

Family photo in front of the historic store, June 2011.

First published in the United States of America in 2014 by
Chronicle Books LLC.
First published in France in 2011 by Hachette Livre (Maramount).

Copyright © 2011 by Hachette Livre (Maramount)
Text copyright © 2011 by Julien Merceron.
Photographs copyright © 2011 by Jean Cazals.
Illustrations copyright © 2011 by Sophie Pechaud and Julie Serre.

Library of Congress Cataloging-in-Publication Data available.
ISBN 978-1-4521-1828-4

Manufactured in China

10 9 8 7 6 5 4 3 2 1

Chronicle Books LLC
680 Second Street
San Francisco, California 94107
www.chroniclebooks.com

Chronicle Books publishes distinctive books and gifts. From award-
winning children's titles, bestselling cookbooks, and eclectic pop
culture to acclaimed works of art and design, stationery, and
journals, we craft publishing that's instantly recognizable for its
spirit and creativity. Enjoy our publishing and become part of our
community at www.chroniclebooks.com.